INVISIBILITY

An extraordinary guide to the art of making oneself invisible to others using techniques drawn from alchemy, Rosicrucianism, medieval magic and esoteric Yoga.

By the same author
LEVITATION
TRAVELLER'S GUIDE TO THE ASTRAL PLANE

Dutch medium forming the *cloud*. From Shrenk-Notzing, *Materializationsphänomene* (1914).

INVISIBILITY
Mastering the Art of Vanishing

by
STEVE RICHARDS

THE AQUARIAN PRESS
Wellingborough, Northamptonshire

First published April 1982
Second Impression December 1982
Third Impression 1984

British Library Cataloguing in Publication Data

Richards, Steve.
  Invisibility.
  1. Occult sciences
  I. Title
  131   BF1623.I/

  ISBN 0-85030-305-2
  ISBN 0-85030-281-1 Pbk

Printed and bound in Great Britain.

Contents

name of the cloud in the Qabalah – Astral Projection – The
experience of a friend – Madame Blavatsky on projection –
The letters of Cagliostro – The mother of Romulus ravished
by a spectre – A materialization from Jacolliot – Clouds
noticed in seances – Ectoplasm – Stages of materialization – A
flower materialized in the *cloud* – The experiment of
palingenesis – M. Du Chesne's experiences – Gaffarel and
Oetinger – Yeats on palingenesis – Alchemical theories about
the *cloud*.

The cloud the basis of more than invisibility – Mysterious
references by Anastratus – Hermes and Sincerus Renatus on
secrecy in occultism – *A Treatise of the Rosie-Crucian Secrets* –
The three principles of matter – Body, Spirit, and Soul – Salt,
Sulphur, and Mercury – Their esoteric meanings – Many
names for the Mercury – The form and the Matter – Physical
and metaphysical realities – Alchemists describe the *cloud* –
The *cloud* as the First Matter – Paradoxical descriptions –
Condensation of the *cloud* into solid matter – Stages of
condensation: the four alchemical elements – The order of
subtle emanation – Matter condenses out of empty space –
Einstein's theory of Relativity – The significance of the
human aura – The *cloud* composed of electrons.

Invisibility just the opposite of visibility – Everything
invisible in darkness – Light a stream of energy bullets – Light
bullets like lead bullets – Two kinds of hardness to light –
Magnetic permeability – Electric permittivity – The relative
system of measurement – Barriers and boundary conditions –
Barriers on the astral plane – Barriers set up unconsciously
during sexual intercourse – Barriers set up deliberately during
ceremonial magic – Transparency and invisibility – H.G.
Wells' *The Invisible Man* – Bending light waves around
yourself – Invisibility by complete absorption – Objections

Acknowledgements

The author is grateful to Llewellyn Publications of Saint Paul, Minnesota, for their permission to quote from Israel Regardie's *The Golden Dawn*, and, as usual, to the staff of the Olcott Library and Research Center in Wheaton, Illinois, for their assistance and for the loan of documents.

1. The Invisibles

It was springtime, the month was March, and although the year was 1623 the people of Paris had already acquired their penchant for good food, good wine, and good conversation. There had been little to talk about recently, however. The king was at Fontainebleau, the war in Germany was going well for the Catholic cause, and the realm was at peace.[1] One could, of course, grouse about the *badauds* who stood about uselessly in the city's streets. The *badauds* were always good for a little early morning grumbling. But on this particular morning they would hardly have mattered. For the night before, the night of 3 March 1623, the city of Paris had been quietly invaded. Not by the hated *boche* or the much-feared English; but by a group of men who claimed magical powers, men who called themselves the *Rosicrucians*.

'For eight years these enthusiasts [had] made converts in Germany,' wrote Charles Mackay, 'but they excited little or no attention in other parts of Europe. At last they made their appearance in Paris, and threw all the learned, all the credulous, and all the lovers of the marvellous into commotion. In the beginning of March 1623 the good folks of that city, when they arose one morning, were surprised to find all their walls placarded with the following singular manifesto:

"*We, the deputies of the principal College of the Brethren of The RoZe-Croix* [sic] *have taken up our abode, visible and invisible, in this city, by the grace of the Most High, towards whom are turned the hearts of the Just. We shew and teach without books or signs, and speak all sorts of languages in the countries where we dwell, to draw mankind, our fellows, from error and from death.*"[2]

According to the *Mercure François*, manuscript copies of the placard were passed round hand to hand, and some were affixed to signposts at crossroads — a fact that could not fail to have some magical significance.[3]

'For a long time this strange placard was the sole topic of conversation in all public places,' says Mackay. 'Some few wondered, but the greater number only laughed at it. In the course of a few weeks, two books were published, which raised the first-alarm respecting this mysterious society, whose dwelling-place no one knew, and no members of which had ever been seen. The first was called a history of *The frightful Compacts entered into between the Devil and the pretended "Invisibles"; with their damnable Instructions, the deplorable Ruin of their Disciples, and their miserable end*. The other was called *An Examination of the new unknown Cabala of the Brethren of the Rose-Cross, who have lately inhabited the City of Paris; with the History of their Manners, the Wonders worked by them, and many other particulars.*[4]

The newsmakers on the Pont Neuf, who published these books, gave the mysterious brethren the name 'the Invisibles'.[5]

These books sold rapidly. Everyone was anxious to know something of this dreadful and secret brotherhood. The *badauds* of Paris were so alarmed that they daily expected to see the arch-enemy walking *in propria persona* among them. It was said in these volumes that the Rosicrucian society consisted of six-and-thirty persons in all, who had renounced their baptism and hope of resurrection. That it was not by good angels, as they pretended, that they worked their prodigies; but that it was the devil who gave them power to transport themselves from one end of the world to the other with the rapidity of thought; to speak all languages; to have their purses always full of money, however much they might spend; to be invisible and penetrate into the most secret places, in spite of fastenings of bolts and bars; and to be able to tell the past and future. These thirty-six brethren were divided into bands or companies: six of them only had been sent on the mission to Paris, six to Italy, six to Spain, six to Germany, four to Sweden, and two into Switzerland, two into Flanders, two into Lorraine, and two into Franche Comte. It was generally believed that the missionaries to France resided somewhere in the Marais du Temple. That quarter of Paris soon acquired a bad name, and people were afraid to take houses in it, lest they should be turned out by the six invisibles of the Rose-Cross. It was believed by the populace, and by many others whose education should have taught them better, that persons of a mysterious aspect used to visit the inns and hotels of Paris, eat of the best meats and drink of the best wines, and then suddenly melt away into thin air when the landlord came with the reckoning. That gentle maidens, who went to bed alone, often awoke in the night and found men with them, of shape more beautiful than the Greek Apollo, who immediately became invisible when an alarm was raised. It was also said that many persons found large heaps of gold in their houses without knowing from whence they came. All Paris was in alarm. No man thought himself secure of his goods, no maiden of her virginity, or wife of her chastity, while these Rosicrucians were abroad. In the midst of the commotion, a second placard was issued, to the following effect:

'If any one desires to see the brethren of the Rose-Cross from curiosity alone, he will never communicate with us. But if his will really induces him to inscribe his name in the register of our brotherhood, we, who can judge the thoughts of men, will convince him of the truth of our promises. For this reason we do not publish to the world the place of our abode. Thought alone, in unison with the sincere will of those who desire to know us, is sufficient to make us known to them, and them to us.'

Though the existence of such a society as that of the Rose-Cross was problematical, it was quite evident that somebody or other was concerned in the promulgation of these placards, which were struck up on every wall in Paris. The police endeavoured in vain to find out the offenders, and their want of success only served to increase the perplexity of the public.[6]

Gabriel Naude, a contemporary writer who lived through these events, says that popular feeling concerning the Rosicrucians built up in France until it was sweeping across the country with the ferocity of a hurricane.[7] All sorts of fantastic rumours were abroad. Henry Neuhusius, who wrote a *Pious and Very Useful Advertisement Concerning the Brothers of the Rose-Cross*, contended that there were three

Rosicrucian Colleges in the whole world. One was in India 'in an isle floating in the sea [!], another in Canada, and the third in the city of Paris, in certain subterranean places'.[8] Some believed that the Invisibles were on the side of God; others the Devil.

'Such was the consternation in Paris,' reported *Chambers' Journal*, 'that every man who could not give a satisfactory account of himself was in danger of being pelted to death; and quiet citizens slept with loaded muskets at their bedsides, to take vengeance upon any Rosicrucian who might violate the sanctity of their chambers.'[9]

The row lasted well into 1624, by which time we may well imagine that the Rosicrucians had long since skipped out of France, as invisibly as they arrived. However, they did not skip out of Europe, and there is evidence that their techniques for making themselves invisible were still taught. Intimations to that effect have been found in the papers left behind by eminent men known to have been Rosicrucian brethren.

One of these was Elias Ashmole, who left a 'recipe how to walk invisible' among the papers deposited at the Bodleian library. Another of these was John Macky, an early Masonic leader – the early Masons were believed to be a resurrection of the old Rosicrucian Order – who taught 'a Masonicall Art, by which any man could (in a moment) render himself invisible'.[10]

Some of these techniques are suspect. For example, there is a supposedly Rosicrucian recipe for invisibility in one of the notebooks of John Aubrey. 'This Receipt,' he wrote, 'is in Johannes de Florentia (a Rosy-Crucian), a book in 8° in high Dutch. Dr Ridgeley the Physitian [sic] hath it, who told me of this.' Now Johannes de Florentia was probably Florentinus de Valentia, and if Aubrey could not even get the name right, one wonders what else might have been garbled. As for the 'Receipt' itself, it reads like something that might have come from a medieval chapbook: 'Take on 'Mid-summer night, at xii, Astrologically, when all the Planets are above the earth, a Serpent, and kill him, and skinne him; and dry it in the shade, and bring it to a powder. Hold it in your hand and you will be invisible.'[11]

Somewhat closer to our time is Francis Barrett, who published *The Magus* in 1801, and who was not afraid to sign his name with the initials

'F.R.C.' He informs us that 'the stone heliotropium, green, like a jasper or an emerald beset with specks ... so dazzles the eyes of men that it will cause the bearer to be invisible.'[12] The very same idea is found in Ben Jonson's play, *The Vnderwood*, in which he speaks of:

> The Chimera of the Rosie-Crosse,
> Their signs, their seales, their hermetique rings;
> Their jemme of riches, and bright stone that brings
> Invisibilitie, and strength, and tongues.[13]

In his Rosicrucian novel, *Zanoni*, Edward Bulwer–Lytton has the Rosicrucian wizard Mejnour claim, among other things, the power 'to disarm and elude the wrath of men, to glide (if not incorporeal) invisible to eyes over which we can throw a mist and darkness', and he says that 'this some seers have professed to be the virtue of a stone of agate. Abaris placed it in his arrow.'[14]

If this was the Rosicrucian method, Lord Lytton would know. Wynn Westcott states that he was enrolled in the Rosicrucian College at Frankfurt-am-Main, but had to withdraw after that college was closed in 1850.[15] In a letter to Hargrave Jennings, Lytton frankly admitted that he was a latter-day member of the Order.[16] However, it would appear that the business about magical stones was really just a blind, intended to mislead the uninitiated, because a still later personality, who, like Lytton, claimed Rosicrucian initiation, was even more explicit.

He was H. Spencer Lewis, the founder of the Ancient and Mystical Order Rosae Crucis in San Jose, California, and he says that invisibility is achieved, not with rocks, but with clouds. He says that 'clouds or bodies of mist ... can be called out of the invisible to surround a person and thus shut him out of the sight of others' and he says that 'this is a demonstration often performed to prove the operation of many Cosmic and spiritual laws.'[17] Interestingly, we recall that Mejnour the wizard learned 'to glide (if not incorporeal) insivible to eyes *over which we can throw a mist and darkness*' (my italics). It would appear that here indeed is the true secret of the Rosicrucians, a fact which is made even more interesting when Lewis says that the 'secret is still in practice in the mystical schools of today'.[18]

There is little doubt that Bulwer himself possessed it, although his experiments were not always successful. According to his grandson, 'he would pass through a room full of visitors in the morning, arrayed in a dressing-gown, believing himself to be invisible, and then appear later in the day very carefully and elaborately dressed, and greet his guests as if meeting them for the first time.'[19] The moral of the tale is obvious: be careful when making yourself invisible, lest you succeed only in making yourself ridiculous.

Even if the technique does not always work to perfection, though, it should be worth knowing, and there is a considerable body of evidence to support the view that the *cloud* is the basis of the Rosicrucian invisibility secret.

In one of the early Rosicrucian manifestos, which was published even before the ruckus in Paris, we read that 'God has so encompassed us about with his *clouds*, that ... we neither can be seen nor known by anybody, except he had the eyes of an eagle.'[20] In an open letter, published somewhat later, we read that the Rosicrucians 'seal up our ears and as it were *cover ourselves up in clouds*' to conceal themselves from those unworthy to join their fraternity.[21]

In the preface to his translation of the Rosicrucian manifestos, Thomas Vaughan says that 'the secret of invisibility was not known to the Dutch boor, nor to his plagiary, the author of *The Manna*; but the Fraternity of R.C. can move in this *white mist*', and he quotes one of their number to the effect that 'Whosoever would communicate with us must be able to see in this light, or us he will never see – unless by our own will.'[22]

In the manuscripts left by the Hermetic Order of the Golden Dawn there is a 'Ritual of Invisibility' in which a similar idea is expressed. The Hermetic Order of the Golden Dawn at least claimed a Rosicrucian basis, although serious doubt has been cast recently by Ellic Howe on that claim, and the idea behind G.D. invisibility is that the Magus should surround himself with a 'Shroud of Darkness and of Mystery'. This shroud is explicitly described as looking like 'a cloud, or veil'.[23]

Now of course the idea here is invisibility through concealment. As

Paracelsus explained it in his *Philosophia Sagax:*

> Visible bodies may be made invisible, or covered, in the same way
> as night covers a man and makes him invisible; or as he would
> become invisible if he were put behind a wall; and as Nature may
> render something visible or invisible by such means, likewise a
> visible substance may be covered with an invisible substance, and be
> made invisible by art.[24]

This idea appears frequently in folklore. The cloud is usually referred
to esoterically as a garment of some kind, which, when worn, conceals
the hero from view. In this category we might place the helmet of
Athena, the cap of Perseus, or the cloak of Manannan.[25] In each case,
the hero surrounds himself with something that causes him not to be
seen, and if we think a moment, it becomes obvious that that
'something' cannot itself be seen. The hero is 'covered' with a garment
that is itself invisible.

In the Buddhist magical text *Patisambhidas* 'to be invisible' is defined
as 'to be covered up and hidden by something; it means to be concealed
and enclosed'.[26] In the *Book of the Sacred Magic of Abra-Melin the Mage*
we find the same ideas.

Abra-Melin tells us to construct certain magic squares and wear them
under our caps whenever we wish to become invisible. The cap is of
course based on the cap of Perseus, and the magic squares are inscribed
with words that have an esoteric significance.

Some of these are words such as TALAC, which means 'thy mists',
or BEROMIN, which means 'coverings or shrouds of concealment'.
Others are NEDAC, 'accumulated darkness', and SIMLAH, 'to clothe
or surround on all sides'. MacGregor Mathers notes that 'all these
names distinctly express some idea related to invisibility'.[27] 'Thy mists'
can only be a veiled reference to the cloud.

As King James I interpreted it, the Magi had to 'thicken and obscure
so the air that is next about them, by contracting it straight together,
that the beams of any other man's eyes cannot pierce through the same,
to see them.'[28] One of his countrymen who is said to have possessed the
secret was Roger Bacon.

Non-occultists know Friar Bacon as the inventor of gunpowder. He was a dreamer who anticipated many modern inventions. In his time, though, his great learning made him suspect to the good Fathers of the Church, and he was accused of trafficking with spirits.

Whatever the truth was, the Rosicrucians claim him as one of their own, and there is evidence that he may have been a student of occultism – of the white variety.

In *The Famous History of Friar Bacon* all sorts of wonders are attributed to him. He is said to have invented a glass wherein one could see anything transpiring anywhere on earth, and a head made of brass which expounded great wisdom. In every recorded instance he used these things for the benefit of mankind, and in one particular story he manifested the power of invisibility.

A certain maiden named Millicent was, it is said, loved by two men – the one an Oxfordshire gentleman, and the other, a knight. The Oxfordshire gentleman won the favour of Millicent, but alas – her father favoured the knight, and a dastardly knight he was, too. He saw that she would never have him by choice, and therefore contrived, with the help of Friar Bungay and her father, that she should have him by knavery. Her father took her for a country drive – or so she thought it was to be. They arrived at a small chapel, wherein waited the knight and Friar Bungay, ready to perform the ceremony. In the meantime the Oxfordshire gentleman learned of all this, and besought the aid of Friar Bacon. Bacon 'bade him be comforted, for he would prevent the marriage. Then, taking the gentleman on his knees, he seated himself in a *magic chair*, which immediately transported them through the air to the chapel.' Once there, Friar Bacon ended the ceremony by striking Friar Bungay dumb, and 'raised such a *mist* in the chapel that *the father could not see his daughter, nor could the knight see either of them.*'[29] While the company were thus confounded, Bacon led the lovers to the chapel door, and there married them himself.

The story has obviously suffered some embellishment over the years, but the reference to a *mist* in connection with invisibility suggests that it may have been based on truth. For this mist really does exist. And it is in fact noticed with certain specific kinds of psychic phenomena –

invisibility being only one. By looking at just what these specific kinds of psychic phenomena are, we can get an insight into what the mist is. And when we know what it *is*, we will know how it can be *produced*.

2. Ectoplasm, and All That

The Rosicrucians may have been the most interesting people to experiment with invisibility and the cloud, but they certainly were not the first. As far back as prehistoric times, the cloud was well known in Greece, and it is mentioned in the writings of both Homer and Hesiod.

In the *Odyssey*, when Odysseus was washed ashore close to the city of the Phaeacians, he wished to make his way to the palace of the city's king to confer with him on certain matters. However, he was an aristocratic soul, and did not wish to be bothered by the common herd of the Phaeacians on the way. Hence, Homer tells us that the goddess Athene 'shed *a deep mist* about Odysseus for the favour that she bare him, lest any of the Phaeacians, high of heart, should meet him and mock him in sharp speech, and ask him who he was.'[1]

As Odysseus passed through the city, 'not one of the Phaeacians could see him … for the great goddess Athene in her good will toward him had hidden him in *a thick cloud of darkness.* '[2]

Odysseus went straight through the court, 'still hidden by the *cloak of darkness* in which Athene had enveloped him, until he reached Arete and King Alcinous. Then did he lay his hands upon the knees of the queen, and at that moment that miraculous darkness fell away from him and he became visible. Everyone was speechless with surprise at seeing a man there.'[3]

In his translation, Samuel Butler uses such phrases as 'a wondrous mist' and 'a thick mist' in translating Homer's original.[4] Still another modern writer uses the phrase 'a magic mist', and points out that there are similar stories in *The Iliad.*[5]

One of these appears in book fourteen. Hera approaches Zeus for some favour, while Homer's heroes are battling over Troy, and is herself asked by Zeus to grant him a sexual favour. The two are atop Mount Ida, there are other gods and goddesses about, and little opportunity for privacy, and Hera is naturally quite embarrassed. She suggests that Zeus might wish to retire to her room, where they could be alone, but the god has a better idea: privacy through invisibility. It is doubtful that a mere mortal could concentrate on occult exercises at a time like *that*, but Zeus did, and Homer says that he surrounded himself and Hera with 'such a dense golden cloud that the very sun, for all his bright piercing beams [could] not see through it'.[6]

Hesiod, another ancient Greek poet, has the same idea in his works, only this time not in connection with a story. Hesiod accepts the ancient myth of the Four Ages of Man — which may not be a myth — and he brings up the *cloud* in connection with the men of the Golden Age. "Now that the earth has gathered over this generation,' he says, 'these are called pure and blessed spirits ... They mantle themselves in *dark mist* and wander all over the country.[7]

In countries other than Greece, the cloud was often mentioned in connection with the final disappearance of a great man from the earth. Everyone has heard the modern cliché that great men never die — they just fade away. In ancient times this was believed quite literally. Rather than dying the way plain mortals do, great men were thought to fade out of sight — in the cloud.

One of these was the Jewish lawgiver, Moses. Jewish historians believe that the historical Moses was murdered by ambitious younger politicians.[8] But there are several stories about the legendary Moses, and one of the most interesting may be found in Josephus' *Antiquities of the Jews*.

As he went to the place where he was to vanish from their sight, they all followed after him, weeping, but Moses beckoned with his hand to all who were remote from him, and bade them stay behind in quiet. All those who accompanied him were the Senate, and Eleazar, the High Priest, and Joshua, their commander. As soon as they were come to the mountain called *Abarim* ... [Moses] dismissed the Senate ... and a *cloud* stood over him on the sudden, and he disappeared.[9]

In certain rabbinical legends, and also in *The Samaritan Book of Joshua*, we find a similar story, with an interesting addition. In some of these newer legends, Moses is said not only to have disappeared in the cloud, but to have ascended to Heaven as well.[10]

With that, we connect with a very common legend indeed. Doane says that not only Moses, but also Buddha, Krishna, Rama, Lao-Kiun, and Zoroaster are said to have ascended to Heaven, and we might add Jesus to the list as well.[11] In The Acts of the Apostles we are told a story about Jesus that is remarkably similar to Josephus' story about Moses. He is said to have ascended the Mount of Olives with his closest disciples, and to have formally bidden them farewell. After that, 'he was taken up, and *a cloud received him out of their sight*'.[12] This passage is usually interpreted to mean that Jesus ascended to the clouds in the sky, and disappeared that way. But H. Spencer Lewis, founder and first Imperator of the Rosicrucian Order (AMORC), believed that the *cloud* spoken of here was a mystical cloud, and that Jesus in fact disappeared on the ground.[13]

Olivier Leroy reached a similar conclusion studying the lives of certain Catholic saints credited with such ascensions: 'It is possible to account for the vanishing of the levitated person ... not by the incredible height reached ... in his ascent ... but by a phenomenon of *invisibility*, some instances of which are to be found in the lives of several saints.'[14]

Hercules, son of Zeus by a mortal mother, is said to have ended his life on a funeral pyre on Mount Oeta, which was lit by a passing shepherd named Poeas. Once again we have the mountain present in the story – no disciples in this case – and as the pyre was burning, we are told that 'a *cloud* passed under Hercules and with a peal of thunder wafted him up to Heaven. Thereafter he obtained immortality.'[15] Commenting on this myth, Galen says that the same was true of Aesculapius, Dionysius, 'and others, who laboured for the benefit of mankind'. They were 'raised to the angels in *a column of fire*', he says, and he assumed that 'God did thus with them in order to destroy the mortal and earthly part of them by the fire, and afterwards to attract to himself the immortal part of them, and to raise their souls to Heaven.'[16] We find this manner of description – of the cloud as 'a column of fire'

– in the story of the Ascension of Elijah, and in modern accounts as well.[17]

The Canadian mystic Richard Maurice Bucke had just such an experience. It came 'all at once, without warning of any kind. [Bucke] found himself wrapped around, as it were, by a *flame-coloured cloud*. For an instant he thought of fire – some conflagration in the great city. The next [instant] he knew that the light was within himself.'[18]

Bucke did not experience the Ascension in the sense of hearing celestial music or seeing heavenly scenes. His experience was not that profound. But he did experience 'a sense of exaltation, of joyousness, accompanied by an intellectual illumination quite impossible to describe'.[19] He was so moved by the experience that he spent the remainder of his life studying in it. He even gave it a special name. He called it *Cosmic Consciousness*.

Prior to that time is was called *enlightenment*, and *illumination* – two words which suggest an experience of light.[20] In *The Secret of the Golden Flower* the experience is given a delightful Chinese name: 'In the empty chamber it grows light'.[21] 'As soon as one is quiet the light of the eyes begin to blaze up so that everything before one becomes quite bright as if one were in a *cloud*. If one opens one's eyes and seeks the body, it is not to be found.'[22]

Cornelius Agrippa speaks of 'a wise man' who 'testified concerning himself that on all sides sparkling flames issued from his body, accompanied even by noise.'[23] In *La Vita Nuova*, Dante claims to have seen such a flame-coloured cloud, and to have had a vision of a man connected with it:

> There appeared in my room *a mist of the colour of fire*, within the which I discerned the figure of a Lord of terrible aspect to such as should gaze upon him, but who seemed therewithal to rejoice that it was a marvel to see. Speaking, he said many things, among the which I could understand but few, and of these this: *Ego Dominus tuus* – I am your Master.[24]

In the Qabalah the 'shining cloud that causes man to have visions' is called *hazaz* – a Hebrew word which is strikingly similar to our

English word *haze*.[25] It happens that these clouds are associated with several different types of psychic phenomena, of which Ascensions and invisibility are only two.

A third, as we can see from Dante's experience, is *astral projection*. Astral projection is an occult phenomenon in which the projector's consciousness seems to leave his body and travel independently through space. Science has written this off as a mere hallucination, although even scientists admit that people *do have* this experience.[26] But occultists maintain that the experience is quite real, and in proof they point to the fact that the projector can sometimes cause a *visible image* of himself to appear at distant places.

Sometimes the image appears when the projector would rather it did not. Many years ago, a friend of mine told me an amusing experience he had in this connection. He had been studying astral projection with a well known correspondence school, and, following the school's instructions, he decided to project to the house of a friend. The friend was a lady, and a co-worker, and, according to the instructions given out in this particular school, he was to wait until the friend would certainly have retired for the night, then visualize himself standing at the foot of her bed. He did so, and immediately felt that he really *was* standing there:

> She was in bed with her husband. He was already alseep, and she was lying there, with eyes half open, waiting to drop off. She saw me, and said 'Oh, go away, Geoffrey, I'm sleeping!' And that was the end of the experience.

The following morning he went to work and sought her out, with the intention of verifying the experience, if it was real. He found her standing about with a large group of other women, and when she saw him, she screamed, and said: 'Geoffrey! You were in my bedroom last night! And I said "Go away, Geoffrey! I'm sleeping!"' Needless to say, my friend has never attempted astral projection since.

Others have, fortunately, and from their experiments it appears certain that the *cloud* is involved somehow whenever visible images are produced. 'An Adept can project and make visible a hand, a foot, or any

other portion of his body,' wrote Madame Blavatsky, 'or the whole of it
... We have seen this done in full day, while [the Adept's] hands and feet
were being held by a skeptical friend. Little by little the whole astral body
oozed out like a *vapoury cloud*, until there stood before us two forms, of
which the second was an exact duplicate of the first, only slightly more
shadowy.'[27]

In one of the letters of Cagliostro, which was confiscated by the
Inquisition at his arrest, and which was written to him by the Master of
one of his Egyptian Lodges, there is a similar report. 'The first
philosopher of the New Testament appeared without being called,' the
letter says, 'and gave the entire assembly, prostrate before *the blue cloud
in which he appeared*, his blessing.'[28] Blue is in fact one of the colours that
the cloud routinely assumes. *The Rosicrucian Manual*, for example,
describes the cloud as 'mistylight' and 'blue-grey'.[29]

Still another story comes from the ancient Roman writer Dionysius
of Halicarnassus. The origin of the story was Ilia, mother of Romulus
and Remus. She was a Vestal Virgin, and, according to the story, was
ravished by someone while she was in a grove consecrated to the god
Mars.

> It is said by some that the act was committed by one of her lovers to
> gratify his passion. Others make Amulius the author of it ... But the
> greatest number give this fabulous account: that it was a spectre,
> representing the god to whom the place was consecrated. They add
> that this adventure was attended, among other heavenly signs, with
> an eclipse of the sun, and a darkness spread over the heavens; that
> the spectre far excelled the appearance of a man, both in beauty and
> in stature; and that the ravisher, to comfort the maiden, commanded
> her to be not at all concerned at what had happened, since she had
> been united by marriage to the genius of the place. Having said this,
> he was *wrapped in a cloud*, and, being lifted from the earth, was borne
> upwards through the air.[30]

The technical name for such a visitation is *incubus*. That a mere
phantom could visit a moral woman, have sexual intercourse with her,
and thus sire children, was a common belief in the Middle Ages. Many

ladies who were unmarried, and who were found to be pregnant one day were able to keep their reputations unsullied by referring to such a being as the cause. Practically every great man who was ever born in ancient times is said to have been spawned in this way – including Plato and Alexander the Great. And if we follow Huysmans – who makes much of the incubus and succubus legends in *Là Bas* – it would appear that the belief was common among peasant-folk in France in the last century.

A perhaps more remarkable yarn appears in one of Jacolliot's books, which, like all Jacolliot's other tales, seems a bit too good to be true, and yet bears unmistakable marks of authenticity. Jacolliot was in the presence of a Hindu *fakir* (pronounced fack-*eer*) who was working a ritual of materialization. The ritual involved the chanting of certain *mantras* and the maintenance of a small brasier of incense, which was done by Jacolliot himself. Suddenly,

A cloud began to hover near the small brasier, which, by request of the Hindu, I had constantly fed with live coals. Little by little it assumed a form entirely human, and I distinguished the spectre – for I cannot call it otherwise – of an ancient Brahmin sacrificator, kneeling near the little brasier.

He bore on his forehead the signs sacred to Vishnu, and around his body the triple cord, sign of the initiates of the priestly castes. At a given moment, he took a pinch of perfumed powder, and threw it upon the coals. A thick smoke arose on the instant, and filled the two chambers.

When it was dissipated, I perceived the spectre, which two steps from me was extending its fleshless hand.

'Art thou, indeed,'' said I at this moment, in a loud voice, 'an ancient inhabitant of the earth?'

I had not finished the question, when the word AM (yes) appeared in letters of fire, on the breast of the old Brahmin, with an effect much like that which the word would produce had it been written in the dark with a stick of phosphorus.

'Will you leave me nothing in token of your visit?' I continued.

The spirit broke the triple cord, composed of three strands of cotton which begirt his loins, gave it to me, and vanished at my feet.[31]

Had Jacolliot been a little more precise, he would have noted that the spirit 'vanished' by being resolved back into the cloud – just the reverse of the process whereby he materialized in the first place.

This kind of precision, however, does not seem to be in the nature of occultists. For that we must needs refer to the modern Spiritualists, or, more precisely, to the scientists who have studied spiritualistic phenomena.

There is no question that the Spiritualists were familiar with the cloud. An E.A. Brackett, who worked with the medium Helen Berry in the USA in 1885, described the formation of 'a small, white, cloud-like substance' which gradually expanded to cover four or five feet, and then formed itself into the image of a woman.[32] In a *séance* with W. Lawrence, Judge Peterson saw what he described as a 'fleecy cloud' which issued from the medium's side, and gradually solidified into a human body. This was in 1887. In still another case, James Curtis described what he saw as a 'cloud-like, white-grey vapour', apparently produced by the medium Slade in Australia in 1878.[33]

Charles Richet, who studied this phenomenon at great length, gave the cloud a special name. He called it *ectoplasm*, because it tends to form itself into apparently living substances – hands and faces – at a distance from the medium's body. Others have called it teleplasm, or ideoplasm, but ectoplasm remains the most popular name.

Richet believed that he could distinguish three or perhaps four definite stages in ectoplasmic formations. The first of these is the stage in which nothing visible has been produced, but raps are heard, objects are perhaps moved about, and sitters feel that they have been touched. The second occurs when the cloud just begins to be visible. An ectoplasmic hand may 'begin to be visible', but it is 'still more or less amorphous'. In the third stage 'a luminous cloud is seen which finally organizes itself and develops into a nude human shape'.[34] In this stage the manifestation is substantial enough to be photographed. In the fourth stage an entire human body – quite substantial – may be materialized.[35]

Now the materialization need not necessarily be of a *human form*. The cloud itself is, after all, quite amorphous. And there is the possibility that it might be shaped into forms non-human and even inanimate. Augustine mentions a somnambulist whose astral body was known to venture forth in animal form while he slept.[36] And there are other stories – mostly from the Far East – of materializations of flowers.

One of these stories comes from Madame Blavatsky, and concerns an experience she had while travelling through Tibet.

Many of the Lamaseries contain schools of magic, but the most celebrated is the collegiate monastery of the *Shutukt*, to which there are attached more than thirty-thousand monks, the Lamasery forming a small city. Some of the female nuns possess marvellous psychological powers. We have met some of these women on their way from Lhasa to Candi, in Ceylon. To avoid the Muslims and other sects, they travel by night, alone, unarmed, and without the least fear of wild animals, for these will not harm them. At the first glimpse of dawn they take refuge in caves and *viharas*, prepared for them by their co-religionists at calculated distances. For notwithstanding the fact that Buddhism has taken refuge in Ceylon, and nominally there are but few of the denomination in British India, yet the secret *Byauds* (brotherhoods) and Buddhist *viharas* are numerous, and every Jain feels himself obliged to help, indiscriminately, Buddhist or Lamaist.

Ever on the lookout for occult phenomena, hungering for sights, one of the most interesting we have ever seen was performed by one of these poor travelling *Biskshunis*. It was years ago, and at a time when such manifestations were new to the writer. We were taken to visit the pilgrims by a Buddhist friend, a mystical gentleman born at Kashmir, of Katchi parents, but a Buddhist-Lamaist by conversion, who generally resides at Lhasa.

'Why carry about this bunch of dead plants?' inquired one of the *Biskshunis*, an emaciated, tall, and elderly woman, pointing to a large nosegay of beautiful, fresh, and fragrant flowers in the writer's hands.

'Dead?' we asked inquiringly. 'Why, they have just been gathered in the garden.''

'And yet they are dead,' she gravely answered. 'To be born in this world – is that not death? See how these herbs look in the World of Eternal Light, in the Gardens of our Blessed Foh.'

Without moving from the place where she was sitting, the Ani took a flower from the bunch, laid it in her lap, and began to draw together, by large handfuls as it were, invisible material from the surrounding atmosphere. Presently, a very, very faint nodule of *vapour* was seen, and this slowly took shape and colour until, poised in mid-air, [it] appeared like a copy of the bloom we had given her. Faithful to the last line and the least petal it was, and lying on its side like the original, but a thousand times more gorgeous in hue and exquisite in beauty, as the glorified human spirit is more beauteous than its physical capsule.

Flower after flower to the minutest herb was thus reproduced and made to vanish, reappearing at our desire – nay, at our simple thought. Having selected a full-blown rose, we held it at arm's length, and in a few minutes our arm, hand, and the flower, perfect in every detail, appeared reflected in the vacant space, about two yards from where we sat. But whole, the flower seemed immeasurably beautified and as ethereal as the other spirit-flowers, the arm and hand appeared as a mere reflection in a looking-glass, even to a large spot on the forearm, left on it by a damp piece of earth which had stuck to one of the roots. Later we learned the reason why.[37]

Those who have been fortunate enough to receive visits from the Master Morya often report that such a materialized flower has been left behind as a token of the visit. But Western occultists have not been entirely left out of the flower business.

In Western occultism this phenomenon is known as *palingenesis*, and usually refers to the materialization of a flower that has been cremated. M. du Chesne claims to have known a Polish physician who lived in Cracovia, and who demonstrated the feat for visitors.

He had a set of small glasses, in each of which was the ashes of a certain type of flower. All of the more common varieties were represented in his collection, and, should one of his visitors wish to see the original flower, the physician had only to hold the glass over the flame of a lighted candle. Says Gaffarel:

So soon as it ever began to feel the heat you should presently see the ashes begin to move, which afterwards rising up and dispersing themselves about the glass, you should immediately observe a kind of little *dark cloud*, which, dividing itself into many parts, came to represent a rose, but so fair, so fresh, and so perfect a one, that you would have thought it to have been as substantial and as odiferous a rose as grows on the rose-tree.[38]

According to Madame Blavatsky, the same deed was done by Kircher, Digby, and Vallemont.

At a meeting of naturalists in 1834 at Stuttgart, a receipt for producing such experiments was found in a work of Oetinger. Ashes of burned plants contained in vials, when heated, exhibited again their various forms. 'A small, obscure *cloud* gradually rose in the vial, took a definite form, and presented to the eye the flower or plant the ashes consisted of.' 'The earthly husk,' wrote Oetinger, 'remains in the retort, while the volatile essence ascends, like a spirit, perfect in form, but void of substance.'[39]

The alchemists compared this phenomenon with the legend of the Phoenix, a mythical bird that was said to arise from its own ashes every five-hundred years, and fly to the sun-temple at Heliopolis, where its appearance was thought by the Egyptians to be a favourable omen.

Not just everyone can achieve the palingenesis experiment successfully, though. W.B. Yeats, whose occult attainments were considerable, believed that it could be done by placing the ashes 'under ... the receiver of an air pump', and by standing 'the receiver in the moonlight for so many nights'. 'The ghost of the flower' was supposed to 'appear hovering over its ashes', but he says that 'I got together a committee which performed this experiment without results.'[40]

Yeats' mistake was in assuming that the experiment was entirely physical, though. Hartmann mentions Kircher, who resurrected such a flower from its own ashes before Queen Christina of Sweden in 1687.[41] And he explains that 'a person who wants to be an alchemist must have in himself the "magnesia", which means the magnetic power to attract and coagulate invisible astral elements. I know from personal observations that [alchemical] prescriptions are not only allegorically, but literally true, and will prove successful in the hands of an alchemist, [but] will only cause a waste of time and money in the hands of one who has not the necessary qualifications.'[42]

Those who *had* those qualifications did what Richet was to do in a later age – experiment intensively. And they learned a good deal about how the cloud works – whence it comes, and how it is formed. Most of all, they learned what the cloud *is*. Their theories – concealed beneath a perplexing veil of alchemical symbolism – baffled the uninitiated for centuries. But their significance has recently been discovered. And it is these theories that we shall take up next.

3. The Mysteries of Alchemy

In the last chapter we saw that forms can not only *dis*-appear in the cloud; they can *appear* in it as well, which gives a clue as to what the cloud really is. It is, as Crawford, said, the basis of all psychical manifestation. But it is something more than that. It is the basis of all *physical* manifestation as well.

That this is so can be seen from the experiment of palingenesis, in which a plant is resurrected from its own ashes. It seemed to the alchemists that for the form of the plant to appear – even in the cloud – the form itself had to exist in the *astral light* after the plant was cremated. They believed that there was an intimate relationship between the astral light and the cloud, and that both were related to the formation of visible matter. In fact, the alchemists were the *only* occultists who tried to understand what the cloud was and what its place in the universe might be. But whereas that solves one problem for us, it creates another, because alchemy is probably the most occult of all the occult sciences.

When Anastratus tells us in the *Turba Philosophorum* that 'the red sand of the sea is the costliest thing in the world', and that 'it is the saliva of the Moon, which is added to the light of the Sun, which coagulates it', he is obviously not speaking to a lay audience.[1] In fact, the alchemists deliberately obfuscated their books. They took an oath on initiation into the secrets of the Art to 'veil their writings in misty speech' which would, as Michael Maier put it, 'instruct the Wise, and further confound the Ignorant'.

'Evil men are unworthy of wisdom,' wrote Hermes in *The Book of the Seven Chapters*. 'These secrets, then, it behoves us to guard and conceal from the wicked world.'[2] In the eighteenth Article of the

Rosicrucian constitution published by Sincerus Renatus in 1710, the brethren were 'forbidden to make public the sacred and secret matter, or any manipulation, coagulation, or solution thereof'.[3]

To give you an idea just how the alchemists kept their secrets secret, let me quote from my favourite example of typically 'alchemical' writing. It comes from an unpublished manuscript in the British Museum, entitled *A Treatise of the Rosie-Crucian Secrets*, attributed, perhaps falsely, to Dr Dee:

> The contemplative order of the Rosie Cross have presented to the world angels, spirits, plants, and metals, with the times in astromancy and geomancy, to prepare and unite them telesmatically. This is the substance which at present in our study is the child of the Sun and Moon, placed between two fires, and in the darkest night receives a light and retains it. The angels and intelligences are attracted by an horrible emptiness, and attend to the astrolasms forever. He hath in him a thick fire, by which he captivates the thin genii. Now I will demonstrate in what thing, of what thing, and by what thing the medicine and multiplier of metals is made. It is even in the nature of metals. In the great Lion's bed the Sun and Moon are born. They are married and beget a king. The king feeds on the Lion's blood, which is the king's father and mother, who are at the same time his brother and sister. *I fear I betray the secret!*[4]

I can quote no more. Obviously, to do so would risk putting too much of the *secret*, here too plainly revealed, into the hands of the uninitiated. But wait; remembering what De Quincey said, how when the weather is fair, philosophers are bound to be good-tempered, I will tell it to you anyway.

The secret is in the language- or perhaps, rather the jargon-itself. As Nicholas Flamel admitted, 'the Philosophers do ordinarily use these terms of Art to hide the secret from evil men'.[5] When Hermes says that 'the division that was made upon the Water by the ancient philosophers separates it into four substances, one to two, and three to one, the third part of which is colour, that is to say, a coagulating moisture' we might think he is speaking nonsense.[6] But that is not true at all. It is a statement full of meaning to the Wise.

Let us start with fundamentals. The alchemists, starting with Hermes, who was the very first of them, contended that matter was threefold: 'Our Stone hath semblably to a man, Body, Soul, and Spirit,' wrote Flamel.[7] And of these three elements, only one – the body – was said to be visible. The other two were invisible, subtle, elements, which are neither known to, nor studied by, orthodox chemistry to this day.

After Geber, in about the eight century A.D., another set of terms became popular: Salt, Sulphur, and Mercury. They meant the same thing as body, soul, and spirit. As Euxodus said: 'There are three different substances, and three natural principles of bodies – Salt. Sulphur and Mercury – which are the spirit, the soul and the body '[8] The alchemists revealed the correspondences between Salt, Sulphur and Mercury in suitably obscure places buried in suitably obscure texts. The following comes from an alchemical poem in German which was published in *The Secret Symbols of the Rosicrucians:*

The *Sal that is Corpus* is the very last in the Art;
The *Sulphur is the soul*, henceforth without which the body can create nothing;
Mercurius is the spirit of power that brings together both body and soul;
Thus is it called a medium, without which nothing can endure.[9]

Now some later writers have assumed that Salt, Sulphur, and Mercury as meant by the alchemists were the kinds of Salt, Sulphur, and Mercury one might buy from a chemical supply house. But the alchemists were very explicit on this point. 'Our Mercury is not the mercury of the vulgar crowd,' one of them wrote.[10] The substances were the Salt, Sulphur, and Mercury of the Wise.

As Eireneus Philalethes wrote in *The Marrow of Alchemy:*

The Matter first of metals Mercury
A moisture is which wetteth not the hand,
Yet flows, and therefore is named Water Dry;
The vulgar is at everyone's command.[11]

It was said to be one substance with a thousand names. In addition to Mercury, the alchemists called it quicksilver, *Mercurius vivus*, Green Lion, Flying Eagle, poison, argent-vive, cambar, aqua permanens, gum, vinegar, wine, sea water, dragon, serpent, and even virgin's milk. Some of the alchemists even considered Sulphur and Mercury to be interchangeable terms, because Mercury was said to contain its own proper Sulphur. All in the interest of confusing the ignorant. As Bloomfield said:

> Our great Elixir, most high of price,
> Our Azoth, our Basilisk, our Cocatrice.
> Some call it also a substance exuberate,
> Some a Mercury of metalline essence,
> Some the Eagle flying with violence,
> Some a Toad for his great vehemence,
> But few or none do name it in kind,
> It is a privy quintessence; keep it well in mind.[12]

Now this use of many different terms for the same thing is nothing unusual in occultism. The astral body has at times been called the sidereal body, the celestial body, the psychic body, the astral double, the phantom, the Beta body, the soul mould, and who knows what else. But whereas modern occultists are merely disorganized, the ancient alchemists were crafty. Their motto was *obscurum per obscurius* – explain the obscure by the more obscure.[13] And yet the Mystery is not so very deep. Because the three substances of the alchemists are the three substances of Aristotle.

Let us try a little experiment in the imagination. Suppose that in your left hand you have a gold coin, and that in your right hand you have a silver coin. And since in your imagination you can imagine anything, let us suppose that these two coins are exactly the same size.

An alchemist will look at your two coins and tell you that there is one similarity and one difference between them. They are both matter – that is the similarity. And they are two different *kinds* of matter – that is the difference.

Now of course, we could say that they have different densities, different specific gravities, different colours. But the alchemist will say that these are *accidental* qualities. All silver is silver-coloured. And all gold has a specific gravity that is peculiar to gold. But there is only one *essential* difference between the two coins, and that is that one coin is gold and one is silver. The accidental qualities all revolve around the one essential nature.

That being the case, Aristotle concluded that there were two principles concealed in matter, which he called matter and form. In the original Greek these were *Hyle* and *Eidos*.

The form of the coins is the 'gold-ness' of the one coin and the 'silver-ness' of the other. In other words, the form of gold is its gold-ness, its quality of being gold, rather than copper, or silver, or tin. The form is quite real, else the coin dealers would not pay you more for your gold coin than for your silver one. And it is also quite consistent; if it were not the Egyptians would have buried their Pharaohs in gold-plated sarcophagi, only to have them dug up again clad in copper or lead. Form is like beauty – real, but non-physical – and for that reason we call it a *metaphysical* reality.

The same thing is true of the 'matter'. You can see a gold coin, but you cannot see the matter that composes it, because pure matter has mass and weight, but no accidental properties and no form. If we could separate the form from the gold coin, we would have a nebulous something with mass but without colour, specific gravity, or any chemical properties. It is rather difficult to imagine something like that, but it is not too difficult to form it. Pure matter is the *cloud*.

'The first something,' says Thomas Vaughan, 'was a certain kind of cloud or darkness.'[14] Pernety describes it as 'like a vapour, or a humid substance, similar to a subtle smoke'.[15]

In *The Twelve Keys* George Ripley describes it as an 'unctuous humiditie'. Urbriger says that it is 'a vapour impregnated with the metallic seed'.[16] Paracelsus says that matter is coagulated smoke, and that the human body is 'vapour materialized by sunshine mixed with the life of the stars'.[17]

Morien of Rome says that the Philosopher's Quicksilver is a 'white vapour' which is also called virgin's milk.[18] And 'Alphidius teaches us that this matter, or this white smoke, is the root of Art, and the Quicksilver of the Sages.'[19]

'It is invisible in nature,' says Vaughan, 'and therefore there are few who find it. Many believe that it is not to *be* found, for the world is made up of many divers dark and particular and contrary qualities, and the first unity is occulted in generation and does not appear.'[20]

It can of course be seen in matter, which is how Aristotle discovered it. But it cannot be seen in itself until it is brought to the edge of visibility.

Now this was the major point of difference between the scholastic philosophers and the fire philosophers. Aristotle and his disciples thought that pure matter was something 'incorporeal and inextended', which is to say, not quite real. It was an abstract concept, but not something that actually existed in nature.

The alchemists, on the other hand, contended that the 'matter' of Aristotle was not only real, but could be demonstrated to exist. 'T'were absurd,' wrote Trevisan, 'to think that gold was formed in the earth perfect in the instant. Something went before. There must be remoter matter.'[21] This same idea is expressed in the *Lucerna Salis*, where we read:

> A certain thing is found in the world
> Which is also in every thing and every place.
> It is not Earth, nor Air, nor Fire, nor Water,
> Albeit it wants none of these.
> For it contains all nature in itself.
> It becomes white and red, is hot and cold,
> It is moist and dry and is diversifiable in every way.
> Only the Band of the Sages have known it ...[22]

After Thomas Aquinas there was a slight change in terminology. What Aristotle called simply matter, Aquinas named *prime* matter. The kind of matter we see all around us he called the *second* matter. It is the result of the union between the prime matter and the form, and is known in alchemy as the *body* of matter, or Salt.

Now the alchemists made one further improvement on this and called Aquinas' prime matter the First Matter. Thus we have the First Matter, the Second Matter, and the form, otherwise known as Mercury, Salt, and Sulphur, or the spirit, the body, and the soul.

Since the soul of matter, or its Sulphur, was responsible for giving it all its characteristics, including colour, the alchemists often called it the *tincture*. This is what Hermes meant when he said that 'the division that was made upon the Water by the ancient philosophers separates it into four substances, one to two, and three to one, the third part of which is colour.'[23] The four are the four elements, the three are the three substances, the one is the Second Matter, and the third part which is colour is the form contained therein.

The First Matter was more interesting. Since it is without 'soul' in its pure form, it was sometimes esoterically called 'dead' matter. And since it was capable of assuming any form and was found in every chunk of visible matter, it lended itself to some delightful paradoxical descriptions.

It can be found in a dunghill. It is the most precious thing in the world, and yet the wisest of men despise it. Children play with it every day, and it can be found everywhere, yet it is nowhere to be seen. Only the Wise know what it is.

Even the Wise were not sure how it got into its visible form, but they thought that the process was one of condensation. In the *Great Art*, Pernety says that the First Matter 'is condensed, more or less, according to the greater or lesser density of the things which it has pleased the Creator to form from it. This mist, this immense vapour, was condensed into a universal chaotic water, which thus became the principle of all [things]'.[24]

Now this word condense means simply 'to make more dense', or 'to bring more matter into a given volume of space'. Returning to our two coins, if we imagine that they are precisely the same size, placing them on a balance, one on the one side, and the other on the other, we shall find that the gold coin is heavier than the silver. Weight has to do with how much matter there is in the coin. Thus if the gold coin weighs more, there is more matter in the gold. And if the two coins are the same size, that means the gold is more dense. The First Matter had to condense more to form gold than it did to form silver.

Another way of looking at it is to consider the condensation of steam to form, first water, and then ice. Water is a more dense form of matter than steam, and ice is more dense than water. Water, steam, and ice represent what scientists call the three states of matter – liquid, gaseous, and solid – and what the alchemists called three of the four elements. Says Albert Poisson:

> In the alchemical theory, the four elements ... are simply states of matter, simple modalities. Water is synonymous with the liquid state, Earth with the solid, Air with the gaseous, and Fire with a very subtle gaseous state, such as gas expanded by the action of heat ... Moreover, elements represent, by extension, physical qualities such as heat (Fire), dryness and solidity (Earth), moisture and fluidity (Water), cold and subtility (Air). Zosimus gave to these the name of *Tetrasomy*.[25]

Now what this tells us is that the process of condensation is not continuous. There are definite stages of development in the process, and one could infer from this that there might be stages even beyond Fire and Air. This is where the First Matter comes in. If we suggest that Air is the most subtle form of the Second Matter, it follows that the next more subtle form after Air would be the First Matter: 'In the *Siva Samhita* this is called "the order of subtle emanation": From the *Akasa* emanated the Air (*Vayu*); from the Air came the Fire (*Tejas*); from Fire, Water (*Apas*); and from Water came the Earth (*Prithivi*).'[26]

Akasa is therefore in Hindu philosophy the equivalent of the First Matter in Western philosophy. It is the state of matter just beyond the gaseous state. And that is important because the Hindus know what *Akasa* is. In his commentary on *The Bhagavad-Gita*, the Maharishi Mahesh Yogi translates the word *Akasa* as space, and that is exactly what it is – empty space.[27]

Now that may seem startling, because it means that space – empty space – can 'condense' to form, first the cloud, then more substantial forms of matter. But this notion is not the exclusive property of the Hindus. It was the contention of Albert Einstein as well.

In his General Theory of Relativity Einstein proved that space – when it contained matter – tended to become warped, curved, bent, and twisted out of shape. This is how he explained the law of gravity. Ordinarily we do not notice these characteristics because their effects are too slight to be visible. Yet this warping must take place, else some of its effects – such as gravity – that we *do* notice, would not exist.

Now Einstein thought that the matter-warps-space theory could be interpreted in either of two ways. Either matter *causes* a warp in space, or matter *is* a warp in space. There is no reason inherent in his equations to favour the one interpretation over the other. And that leads to an interesting discovery. It solves the Mystery of Matter. You and I are just a couple of dimples in the infinite nothingness.[28]

Of course Einstein's equations are far more sophisticated than anything the ancient Hindus were able to produce. But it is an amazing tribute to the Science of Yoga that these ancient philosophers were able to accurately anticipate such an advanced idea. Nonetheless, it leaves us with an interesting paradox: how can nothing at all be warped?

The answer is of course that space is not 'nothing'. If it were, the creation of matter out of space would be creating something out of nothing. If space is something, and not nothing, as it appeared to the Hindu philosophers, then it would have to 'give way' to matter that is placed in it. This would produce a warping in the vicinity.

Put the palms of your hands together in front of you, and then draw them about six inches apart. Your hands are now separated by space. Of course, it is true that there is air between them, but even if you performed this experiment in a vacuum, it is obvious that your hands would still be separated. And if they are separated, they must be separated by something. To say that space is nothing is the same thing as saying that your hands are separated by nothing, and that is the same thing as saying that there is nothing separating your hands, which literally means they are *not* separated. If we insist that space is nothing, we are forced into an absurd philosophical position.

What space *is* is that portion of the Astral Plane closest to the physical. Since space is not material we cannot really see it, but since it is close to the Material Plane we can sense its existence. In our normal state of consciousness space is a paradox. In altered states of consciousness it can actually be 'seen'.

Now there is of course a gap between empty space and substantial matter, and that forces us to look for some intermediate condition. One does not get from one extreme to another without passing through some middle ground, and the middle ground between space and matter appears to be the *cloud*.

Gifted psychics can see a cloud-like haze surrounding pieces of fully formed matter, at the surface, the boundary between solid matter and space. An early Theosophical writer observed that 'all objects exhale from their periphery a sort of *vapour* or *cloud*', and he likened this to a 'localized atmosphere'.[29] It appears that every piece of matter in the universe is still surrounded to some extent with the cloud from which it was originally formed, and that the transition between the surface of the object and the space surrounding it is not abrupt, but betrays the existence of the intermediate condition represented by the cloud. In *Man Visible and Invisible*, C.W. Leadbeater describes the *human aura*, which appears at the surface of the human body, as 'an egg-shaped *cloud* of diaphanous mist', and similar language has been used by every student of the aura since Kilner.[30]

If we search the wisdom of science for some idea of what the cloud could therefore be, we see that it is a cloud of electrons. According to *The Rosicrucian Manual*, electrons are 'the first form into which spirit essence concentrates preparatory to material manifestation'.[31] 'Spirit essence' is just the 'spirit' of the alchemists. The Mercury of the Wise. The First Matter. And as the *Manual* explains, this 'essence, when stressed under certain conditions, gathers into very minute focal points of electrical charge'.[32] These are what we mean by *electrons*.

These electrons by themselves have no chemical characteristics of any kind, although when they are formed into atoms they may take on any chemical 'form' imaginable. They do, however, possess mass. To be specific, one electron has 9.107×10^{-31} kilograms of mass. One can therefore speak of *quantity* in connection with the electron, but not quality. They possess, in short, every one of the traditional attributes of the First Matter.

Since electrons are the building blocks of the atom, and since the atom is the building block of ponderable chunks of matter, one can easily see how a 'cloud' of electrons could be formed into solid matter by mind power. But what you may not see is how such a cloud could make a human being invisible. To understand that, we are going to have to leave chemistry for a while, whether it is occult chemistry or otherwise, and take a look at the nature of light.

4. How You See It, How You Don't

The fact that the cloud is a cloud of electrons is the key to its power of making things invisible. Scientists know that such a cloud of electrons will absorb all light waves entering it, reducing the magnitude of reflected light to zero, and effectively concealing whatever it surrounds. In this chapter I am going to explain just how all that works. The average person is not scientifically trained, and when you start trying some actual experiments in invisibility, I want you to know not only *what* you are to do, but precisely *why* you are to do it.

If I may pervert the meaning of an old-occult expression, I might also say to you: 'to know the invisible, first know the visible'. The occultist who originated that phrase did not mean it in quite the sense that I do, but the intent is valid in either case. There is something to be said for the view that before you learn to make something concealed, you should understand how it could be made manifest in the first place.

Let us begin with a few elementary observations. Suppose that you are sitting in a totally darkened room. The room is full of objects of various kinds, but there is no source of illumination. Everything in the room is in darkness, and, consequently, everything in the room is invisible.

You conclude that light is necessary for visibility to take place, and you draw from your pocket a small pencil flashlight. As soon as you turn your flashlight on, the room becomes visible. You have just entered a light source into the room. Moreover, whatever you shine your flashlight *on* becomes visible as well, whereas those objects that remain in darkness are still concealed.

Now these are common observations, but by analyzing them carefully, we may reach some conclusions that are not so common. We conclude first of all that light is necessary to sight. After all, the eyes are light-sensitive organs. And we conclude that the flashlight is visible in an otherwise darkened room because it is a light source. What might not be so obvious is that whatever you shine your flashlight on becomes visible by the same process. It, too, becomes a light source, by the process known as reflection.

When light is shined upon an object three things can happen: it can be reflected, it can be refracted, and it can be absorbed. The easiest way to understand these is by analogy.

Imagine that you own a rifle and that you like to take it out into the countryside for target shooting. If you shoot at the Greater London Telephone Directory, it is likely that the bullet from your rifle will be absorbed by the book. If you shoot at a cream puff, it is likely that the bullet will pass through without hindrance. And if you shoot at the face of a granite cliff, it is likely that the bullet will ricochet and come back towards you.

The difference is of course the difference in the relative hardnesses of the three targets. The granite cliff is extremely hard to lead bullets. The cream puff is extremely soft. And the Greater London Telephone Directory is somewhere in between. Therefore, the cliff does not allow any penetration whatsoever and the cream puff does not offer any hindrance, whereas the telephone directory allows some penetration with some resistance to the bullet's passage.

Now the same thing happens with light. Light is a stream of bullets that scientists call photons. They are not made of lead the way rifle bullets are. Scientists believe that they are minute packets of energy. But they behave in the same way as lead bullets. When light bullets strike against something that is extremely hard they bounce off. When they hit something that is extremely soft they pass through. And when they hit something in between they are absorbed.

The situation is a little bit more complicated here because light, unlike lead, is a dual phenomenon. Light is both electric and magnetic

– hence the word *electromagnetic*. And anything you shine a light on has two softnesses as far as light is concerned. The electric softness is called the *permittivity*, and the magnetic is the *permeability*.

Both of these qualities can be measured for any substance, and, just as we measure petrol in gallons and distance in miles, so we measure permeability in henries per metre and permittivity in farads per metre. We rarely ever use these units, though, because both of these are usually expressed in relative, and not absolute, terms.

You will recall that in the last chapter we said *Akasa*, or space, is a form of matter. In fact, it is the First Matter. It is the matrix from which more substantial forms of matter originate. And that being the case, even though we do not usually think of *Akasa* as being a form of matter, it has some material characteristics, including a characteristic permittivity and permeability all its own.

The permittivity of *Akasa* is 8.854×10^{-12} farads per metre, and the permeability is 1.256×10^{-6} henries per metre.[1] These are the standards by which relative permittivities and permeabilities are measured. For example, the permeability of water is 1.25598×10^{-6} henries per metre.[2] But that happens to be 99.999% of the permeability of water. So, if I wish I can say that the permeability of water is .99999, and avoid the complicated numbers and the not-so-meaningful units. Using the same system, the permeability of aluminum is 1.000021, the permeability of cobalt is 250, and the permeability of soft iron is 5000. Thus I not only know what the permeabilities of these three *are*, but I also know approximately where they stand relative to empty space – *Akasa*. Aluminium has a permeability pretty close to that of *Akasa*, whereas soft iron has a permeability 5000 times as great. That would not be so obvious were I using absolute numbers. And it helps us to understand why soft iron and cobalt are magnetic materials.

If you wish, you may apply the very same system to permittivities. Air has a permittivity of 1.00059, whereas the permittivity of glass may range from 3.8 to 6.8, depending on how it is manufactured. Rubber has a permittivity of 3. Nylon is 3.5.[3]

Before we can understand how these two softness factors affect light, though, we must combine them into one number which characterizes a particular substance, and we do this by dividing permeability by permittivity and take the square root. The result is a number that scientists call the *complex intrinsic impedance*.

Broadly speaking, complex intrinsic impedance is a hardness factor. The greater the complex intrinsic impedance of substance X, the 'harder' it will appear to light bullets. And it is when there is a sudden change in this hardness that light bullets begin to bounce back – to be reflected. This kind of sudden change is called a *boundary condition*, and boundary conditions are essential for reflection – and visibility – to take place.

This is easy to understand. Suppose that you are having your morning run and that, being inclined to let your mind wander, you don't watch where you are going. As a result, you run straight into a brick wall. The surface of the wall is a boundary condition, and the phenomenon of your body bounding off it is *total reflection*.

The word impedance means literally 'a tendency to impede', and it is obvious that the brick wall has a greater tendency to impede your body than empty space. The exact place where the change of impedance takes place is the surface of the wall, and we therefore say that the surface of the wall is where the boundary condition is found. It is also at the surface of the wall that the total reflection of your body therefrom is initiated.

Now boundary conditions may be different for different kinds of energy. Bulletproof glass is transparent to light bullets, but opaque to lead ones. Occultists know that substances which are opaque to both light bullets *and* lead bullets may be transparent to the astral body. The same physical laws apply in any case.

This is why a person doing astral projection has no need to open doors. He may simply pass through unopened doors that would obstruct his dense, physical body. And the opposite is also true. He may discover obstacles to his astral body that would present no problem at all to the physical.

J.H. Brennan gives an interesting example of this in his book *Astral Door-Ways*. His wife had a spontaneous experience with astral projection while dropping off to sleep one night, and, finding herself 'out of the body', as it were, decided to visit some friends who lived several miles away. She made it to the friends' house, entered, and mounted the stairs to the bedroom. But halfway up the stairs she was stopped. She had a strong suspicion that the couple were engaged in sexual intercourse and that, in Brennan's words, 'it would be wrong to enter the bedroom in such circumstances'.[4] Her sense of propriety was not the only thing stopping her, though. Brennan says that 'she experienced the conviction as a physical barrier. It was almost as if a solid wall had been built across the stairs.'[5]

This is an example of an astral barrier that did not 'exist' on the physical plane. It was undoubtedly created unconsciously by the two lovers as an expression of their desire for privacy. The fact that it was experienced independently by a third person proves that it had objective existence, but not physical existence. To more dense, physical energies, no boundary condition would have existed. Had Mrs Brennan mounted the stairs in the physical, rather than the astral, she could have entered the bedroom *whatever* the couple were doing. She might not even have suspected that such a barrier had been set up.

Those who are foolish enough to try to evoke demons and spirits using ceremonial magic make deliberate use of these principles for self-defence. They draw three circles on the floor, fortify them with certain divine names in Hebrew, and try to erect astral barriers in the places marked with certain banishing rituals. If they are successful, a very real astral barrier will exist, which is no impediment whatever to the physical bodies of the magician and his assistants, but which will stop any spirit who approaches from the astral plane. It may be that such an astral barrier separates Heaven from Hell – who knows?

Now when light bullets strike against such a barrier, or boundary condition, they behave somewhat differently from lead bullets. Fire a stream of lead bullets at a granite cliff, and you will have a stream of lead bullets coming back toward you. But fire a stream of light bullets at a boundary condition – say, an opaque object – and *a certain percentage* of them will be reflected. Some of them will pass through the barrier.

If this were not true, all of us would be blind. Anyone who has had the pleasure of looking at a snow-covered landscape at night knows that the Full Moon delivers enough light to read by. One can see quite easily at night when there is snow on the ground, and during the day it is sometimes necessary to take precautions against eye damage.

This is so because snow reflects most of the light that strikes against it. It is quite 'hard' to light bullets. But most substances are somewhat softer. More light bullets tend to make it through the boundary condition, which means that fewer are reflected.

Just how many are reflected depends on how close the complex intrinsic impedance of substance X is to the complex intrinsic impedance of the surrounding space. The complex intrinsic impedance of the *Akasa* is 377 ohms.[6] The closer the impedance of substance X is to 377 ohms, the less light will be reflected. The further away it is from 377 ohms, the more light will be reflected.

If substance X has an impedance of exactly 377 ohms, *no* light would be reflected. It would all either be absorbed or refracted. And zero reflection means zero visibility. A substance with a complex intrinsic impedance of 377 ohms will never be a light source. It will be invisible.

That this is possible can be seen with glass. A few years ago, when sliding glass patio doors were all the rage in California, home-builders were forced to adopt simple strategies to make the doors more "visible". Homeowners were routinely charging through these doors – which cannot be seen if they are very clean – and seriously injuring themselves. To prevent this, developers would affix small decals to the doors, or mount handles on them which were made of opaque materials.

In *The Invisible Man*, H.G. Wells created a character who made his body transparent, like glass, and made himself invisible that way. But glass is not invisible because it is transparent. It is invisible because it does not reflect light. Most opaque substances do reflect light, but if there were one that did not, it would be just as invisible as glass. It would not be transparent, but you do not have to see through anything for it to be invisible. Remember our darkened room. Everything in the room is invisible whether it is transparent or not. For us to make our bodies transparent would require a radical change in our body chemistries. If we could do such a thing – and I am not ruling it out – it would probably be a one-time experiment.

A second possibility that has been raised by some science-fiction authors is bending light waves around ourselves. If no light waves actually struck against our bodies, none would be reflected. But there are some difficulties with this. One of these is that light usually travels in straight lines, whether we want it to or not. There are of course ways of bending it. Everyone has seen the old pencil-in-a-glass demonstration. You simply fill a glass half-full with water and immerse a pencil in it, so that part of the pencil is in the water, and part out of it. If you then look at the pencil, it appears to have been bent. But the truth is, the *light waves* have been bent. Light tends to slow down when it passes from space into water, and when it slows down light travels in curved – and not straight – lines.

The pencil is still visible, though, and it is difficult to see how we could make use of this effect to make it *in*-visible. That brings us to the third possibility: total absorption.

Total absorption means precisely what the name implies. Light waves still strike the human body, but they are not reflected from it. Since they do not pass all the way through – the human body is not transparent – they are absorbed.

There are difficulties here as well, though, and one of these was aptly stated by J.H. Brennan in his *Experimental Magic*. Mr Brennan doubts that the experiment will even work. 'You may not be able to see the object,' he says, but 'you will certainly be able to see that something is badly wrong.'[7] So it would appear.

Reginald Scot raises the same objection in his *Discoverie of Witchcraft*. 'If they say, as M. Mal. Bodin and many others do affirm, that [the Adepts] are covered with a *cloud* or *veile*, yet methinks that we should see either the covering or the thing covered.'[8]

The question here, though, is not whether we can *see* it, but whether we would want to look at it. The cloud *is* visible – slightly – but it is not something that simply commands attention.

Mr Brennan himself stated the solution to the paradox in *Experimental Magic*. 'If you walked into a room which contained, let's say, Miss [Brigitte] Bardot in a bikini,' he points out, 'you might be forgiven if you failed to notice me sitting quietly in a corner.'[9] The same thing would be true if Miss Bardot were completely dressed. Because women are at the top of what we might call the *visual interest hierarchy*. Women and men both find women more interesting to look at than men. And even a homely woman would be noticed first by someone just entering the room.

In a room full of all men, a person just entering will notice a man before noticing something lower down on the visual interest hierarchy. A man will therefore be noticed before a cat or a dog. A cat or a dog will be noticed before a plant will. And a plant will be noticed before an inanimate object, such as a piece of furniture.

What will not be noticed at all is a condition in the atmosphere which makes it somehow difficult to see. You may notice that something is 'badly wrong', as Mr Brennan puts it. But you will not find the fact fascinating. And you will likely glance away to something more interesting without giving it a thought. Reginald Scot is quite correct in saying that we may see the covering. But he is wrong in assuming that we would want to look at it.

Now it is obvious that if light is absorbed by a material – say, an opaque substance such as a piece of wood – it is absorbed by the atoms of that material. And since atoms are composed of electrons, it follows that electrons have something to do with the absorption process.

Scientists say that specifically the *outer electrons* in the atom absorb light, and they have a name for these. They call them *valence electrons*.

Now because of certain complex laws, the valence electrons in a piece of wood may absorb only those photons which have a certain minimum amount of energy associated with them. For example, if I have an electron whose minimal requirement is 2 electron-volts and a photon appears which has only 1.5 electron-volts, it will not be absorbed. However, if another photon appears which has 3 electron-volts of energy, it *will* be absorbed. It easily meets the minimum requirement.

When its energy is absorbed, the photon ceases to exist. It is like taking all the rubber out of a rubber ball. A photon is nothing but a packet of energy. Take all the energy out of it and there is no photon any more.

Now different photons have different energies because they are not all the same colour. There are green photons, yellow photons, red photons, and even blue photons. Each of these colours is associated with a certain rate of vibrations per second, and a German scientist named Max Planck discovered that these rates of vibration were directly proportional to the photon energy in electron-volts.

We can get the photon energy by multiplying the rate of vibrations in vibrations per second by a number called *Planck's constant*. But we have a problem here because Planck's constant is usually given in *joules*, and not electron-volts. The constant is 6.63 x 10^{-34} joules. A joule is a much larger unit of energy than an electron-volt, and when we express photon energy in joules, we get all kinds of complicated numbers.

That is why electron-volts are preferred. A red photon, for example, has a photon energy of 3.08295 x 10^{-19} joules but only 1.9 electron-volts. It is the same energy in either case, but the electron-volt unit produces simpler numbers that are easier to work with. To get photon energy in electron volts, we simply multiply .0041375 by the photon's rate of vibrations in trillions of vibrations per second. Thus, to get the energy of the red photon, we multiply .0041375 by 465, since a red photon has a rate of vibration of about 465 trillions per second.

Using information in Madame Blavatsky's *Secret Doctrine*, I have compiled the following chart:

	Rate of Vibrations (Trillions/Second)	Photon Energy (Electron-Volts)
Deep Red	465	1.924
Red	484	2.002
Red-Orange	503	2.081
Orange	514	2.126
Yellow	544	2.250
Green	550	2.275
Blue-Green	610	2.523
Blue	631	2.610
Blue-Violet	668	2.763
Violet	708	2.929
Ultraviolet	759	3.140

An atom of silicon has an energy gap of 1.1 electron-volts. That means that a photon striking a silicon atom will have to have an energy of at least 1.1 electron-volts to be absorbed. Since the lowest energy that we see on the chart is 1.924 electron-volts, we would expect silicon to absorb photons of any colour.

If we posit the existence of an atom with an energy gap of 2.2 electron-volts, though, we can see that orange, red-orange, and red photons would be either refracted or reflected, whereas photons with faster rates of vibrations would be absorbed. This is part of the reason why objects have colours.

We can also see from the chart that ultraviolet photons have the highest energies of all. This is why when you are sunbathing, it is the ultraviolet photons from the sun that burn your skin. They have the most energy. It is also why if you leave you car in the sun for long periods of time, your exterior paint will gradually deteriorate. Ultraviolet photons have the power, because of their energy, to break chemical bonds. The dullness in your paint job is the result of a chemical reaction.

Now if electrons have the power to absorb light photons when they are bound into atoms, there is no reason why they should not have the same power when they are free. And the cloud, as we saw in the last chapter, is just a cloud of free electrons. Since the energy gap of the cloud is apparently quite small, *all* the photons that enter it are absorbed, whereas some are usually reflected from more ordinary substances. And with zero reflection, we get, as we have said before, zero visibility.

Now, let us pick up a few more facts about vision. I am now going to tell you how to extend your own sight, so that things that are normally invisible can be seen, after which I shall outline the actual procedures for forming the cloud and making yourself, or anything else, invisible. What is now theory will then become fact.

5. How to Extend Your Sight

Before I get into the practical details of obscuring everyone else's sight, let me tell you something about extending your own. After all, visibility is just the opposite side of *in*-visibility. And you will find that in the study of extending sight you will get some valuable insights into the process of obscuring it.

'Keenness of sight has achieved instances transcending belief in the highest degree,' wrote Pliny. 'Cicero records that a parchment copy of Homer's *Iliad* was enclosed in a nutshell. He also records the case of a man who could see 123 miles. Marcus Varro also gives this man's name, which was Strabo, and states that in the Punic Wars he was in the habit of telling from the promontory of Lilybaeum in Sicily the actual number of ships in a fleet that was passing out from the harbour at Carthage.'[1]

The normal human eye in good health is capable of detecting the light of a match on a clear, dark night at a distance of fifteen miles. It is capable of detecting the light of a candle at a distance of thirty miles![2] When a person who is not night-blind passes from a brilliantly lighted room into one that is dimly lit, his eyes may become as much as 2000 times more sensitive to light. The eye is the basis of the most important of all man's five senses, and is one of the most extraordinary organs in the human body.

Nonetheless, many people have difficulty with their eyes. Possibly as many as half the young adult population cannot see well without corrective lenses, and with age the number increases. The majority of older people suffer from what is called 'middle-aged sight', or *presbyopia*, which is caused by atrophy of the ciliary muscle in the eye and by a gradual hardening of the crystalline lens that is used for focusing.

There is something strange about this, because every other organ in the human body seems to be capable of self-repair, especially in young people. As the doctors say, *medicus curat, natura sanat:* the doctor treats, nature heals. Only the eye is exempted from this privilege, and only the eye must, in every case, be fitted with what one professional in the field called 'those valuable crutches' – spectacles.

This seems strange to an occultist, who is accustomed to questioning orthodox theories about this and that, but it also seemed strange to at least one oculist – a New York oculist named William Horatio Bates.

Bates' arguments were all based on the fact that the orthodox theory was first proposed by Helmholz in the last century. He believed that focusing in the eye – which is technically called *accommodation* – was due entirely to the ciliary muscle and to the crystalline lens, which it controls. If you want to see something far away, for example, the ciliary muscle tends to relax, allowing the lens to flatten. This brings distant scenes to a sharp focus on the *retina* of the eye, which is composed of light-sensitive cells. If you want to see something close up, the muscles tend to tighten, causing the lens to bulge. ·

Dr Bates pointed out, though, that some ability to accommodate has been noticed in cataract patients who have had their lenses totally removed. This is an astonishing fact that cannot be explained in terms of Helmholz's theory, and Dr Bates therefore concluded that Helmholz's theory was either inadequate or positively incorrect.

He suggested instead that the six external muscles that you use when you look up or down or to the right or left have a part to play, by changing the shape of the eye.

A near-sighted person, for example, has an eye that is slightly elongated, so that images come to a focus in front of the retina, instead of on it. The ciliary muscle and lens cannot correct for so great an error of refraction, and corrective lenses are therefore necessary. Concave lenses are required for near-sightedness, and convex lenses for farsightedness, depending on whether the retinal image needs to be moved forwards or backwards.

Dr Bates believed, though, that the external muscles might be pulling the eye out of shape in a person with visual problems, and that if that situation could be corrected, the person might be able to see normally without any corrective lenses at all. If that is true, it means the end of a large and prosperous industry. And that being the case, it is not surprising that Bates' theories found little favour with the makers of optical glass.

An intense advertising campaign was initiated to convince people that they needed to continue buying spectacles for ever and ever. It was pointed out that some of Bates' theories were pretty wild, and it was suggested on that basis that his methods would not work.

The fact is, though, that they *do* work. Eye expert Harris Gruman, who assessed both Bates' theories *and* methods, wrote that 'in spite of his hypotheses and theories, [Bates] did hit upon some worthwhile methods of aiding human sight. Time has proved their worth, and for that the world should be grateful.'[3]

Lawrence Galton mentions a woman who had only one-tenth of normal vision, and who could therefore be considered almost blind. After a few months of visual training she passed a driving test with 20/40 vision. In two years her vision was completely normal.

Another of Galton's examples is a 'far-sighted businessman' who could not read without glasses. The printed word was a mere blur to him. Yet after three months of Bates' training, he discovered that his glasses were no longer necessary. He discarded them and has not used them since.[4]

One of the most interesting testimonials, however, comes from an article in the *Deutsche Medizinische Wochenschrift*. The author was a German Army surgeon who presided over a test of Bates' methods with near-sighted recruits. The recruits were asked to discard their glasses temporarily, and try to pass their marksmanship tests using Bates' exercises instead. The results were so excellent that visual training was officially endorsed by the German government.[5]

The basis of it is quite simple: sight consists of three processes — sensing, selecting, and perceiving. Only the first of these — sensing —

has anything to do with the eyes. Selecting and perceiving takes place entirely in the brain.[6]

In fact, even sensing involves the brain to an extent, because accommodation, *however* it is performed, requires that the brain controls the necessary muscles. After sensing has taken place, the brain must aright the image projected on the retina. The retinal image is upside down. And there must be other corrections in the visual image – again performed by the visual centres in the brain.

'The optical quality of the human eye is extraordinarily bad,' writes Lyall Watson. 'The image projected onto the retina is blurred at the edges, and fades away into iridescent halos. All these defects are put right in the brain.'[7] That being the case, it is obvious that the brain must be in good working order for vision to proceed unimpaired. And that is where Bates comes in. He contends that, owing to stress, our brains *are not* always in good working order.

'The origin of any error of refraction,' he wrote, 'is simply a thought – a wrong thought – and its disappearance is as quick as the thought that relaxes.'[8] Bates mentioned a young man who happened to be twenty-five years old and who was one of his patients. If he stared at a blank wall 'without trying to see' he showed no error in refraction. But if someone caused stress, for example, by saying that he was twenty-six instead of twenty-five, he became near-sighted. 'When he stated or remembered the truth his vision was normal,' wrote Bates. 'But when he stated or imagined an error he had an error of refraction.'[9]

When this was first published the world was astonished. But since then we have learned that stress – the very same thing that appears to cause visual problems – is also responsible for high blood-pressure, heart disease, allergies, asthma, stomach ulcers, and possibly even cancer. It is worth mentioning here that two of these – heart disease and cancer – between them are responsible for three out of every four deaths in the Western world today. It is therefore not surprising if stress affects such a delicate sense as that of sight.

Although we do not normally notice these effects, our ancestors did, and they made them a part of our folklore. Aldous Huxley collected numerous examples. Fear makes the world 'go black' or 'swim before our eyes'. We are 'numb with worry'.[10] There is the proverbial sempstress who can see to thread a needle, but who cannot see to read.[11] And there is the following well-known effect, mentioned by Arthur Edward Waite in *The Mysteries of Magic:* 'If a man be bidden to look for anything by another whose will dominates but perturbs his own, and whom he fears to displease, his anxiety to find it will sometimes so confuse him that he will not see the object, though it may be under his very eyes.'[12]

There are several ways in which you may reverse that process. Dr Forbes Winslow quotes a 'distinguished oculist' to the effect that 'light is injurious to the eyes in proportion as the *red and yellow rays* prevail'.[13] These produce what he calls 'cerebral and visual excitement' – stress in modern language – 'followed by debility of the retina'. Lamp shades which favour calming and soothing colours, such as blue, produce less stress, and better sight.

Another technique is what Bates called *central fixation*. The average reading distance is fourteen inches. And the best clarity is attained within a circle one-half inch in diameter. This is the part of the printed page which produces an image at the exact centre of the retina. The central portion of the retina is called the *macula lutea*, and the centre of the *macula lutea* is called the *fovea centralis*.

Since it is in this one-half inch circle that you can see best, it is obvious that you want to direct your eyes so that whatever you want to see produces an image in that area. Your brain has to work harder to resolve images at the edge of the retina. That produces strain, which causes an error in accommodation, which produces more strain, and so on. Therefore, when you are looking, you need to be sure that you are looking directly at whatever you are looking at. Simple as this principle is, it does not occur to many people who are not trained in optics.

To encourage central fixation, Bates recommended mobility drills and swinging. The next time you are walking along the street, glance at the people on the other side of the street. Glance directly at the first person, then allow your eyes to smoothly pass from that person to the next, and the next, and the next. Each time, look directly at your target.

After you have tried that, try moving your eye back and forth so that you get the illusion of things 'swinging' from side to side. This is essentially a relaxation exercise. Avoid staring, keep your eyes level as you swing, and allow yourself to blink. Blinking not only relaxes the eye, but helps to keep it clean, and by swinging you can get the idea of calmly looking without strain.

Now I am only going to cover one more Bates exercise here. It is the one which is most interesting to occultists. Those who wish to work with the complete Bates system will do well to get one of the excellent manuals that have been published. Especially recommended is Aldous Huxley's *The Art of Seeing*. Not only was it written by one of England's great men of letters, but it is widely available in the public libraries. As for us. I should recommend *palming* even to those who have 20/20 vision.

Like swinging, palming is a relaxation exercise. Unlike swinging, it is done with the eyes closed, usually after any other eye exercises.

What you must do is cover your closed eyes with the palms of your hands. Your eyes should be relaxed, and there should be no tension either in your hands, or in the muscles in your face. You should not rub your eyes with your palms. Just allow your palms to lightly touch your eyelids, and as you do this, visualize a sea of blackness.

Bates says that to the extent that you do not see blackness while palming, you are suffering from mental stress and consequent strain. 'When you can palm perfectly,' he wrote, 'you will see a field so black that it is impossible to remember, imagine, or see anything blacker, and when you are able to do this your sight will be normal.'[14] One of Bates' patients suffered from astigmatism and incipient cataract. He was seventy years old, and effected a complete cure after palming continuously for twenty hours. Aldous Huxley recommends mental palming when the normal method is impossible. Simply close your eyes and imagine that you have covered them with your palms. It is not as effective as actually using your hands, of course, but extremely beneficial nonetheless.[15]

Now the reason that this works, according to Huxley, is that 'all parts of the body carry their own characteristic potentials'. He suggests that 'the placing of the hands over the eyes does something to the electrical condition of the fatigued organs'.[16] According to occultists, he is absolutely right.

Edwin Babbitt anticipated many of Bates' ideas in his *Principles of Light and Colour*. He suggests that 'a person strongly charged with vitalizing force may sometimes animate and regulate these muscles [in the eye] with the ends of the fingers ... I have cured inflamed eyes by placing cool wet fingers over [them].'[17] For problems relating to the optic nerve rather than the eye itself, Babbitt recommends 'a magnetic hand, laid on each anterior portion of the temples, a little back of the eye'.[18] It is a well-known principle of mesmerism that the hands, and especially the fingers, are points at which magnetic energy is concentrated. Eliphas Lévi said that the Astral Light is 'projected' from the thumbs and palms.[19]

The AMORC Rosicrucians teach their members to 'palm' using only the first finger of each hand, on the theory that this is where the 'radial nerve' terminates. I have met several AMORC members who have worked with this technique, and who were eventually able to discard their glasses using this method alone. One of these, a South American, had his progress monitored by an opthalmologist, who confirmed that his eyesight was indeed improving. After you have allowed your forefingers to rest lightly on your closed eyelids for five or ten minutes, you will find it helpful to remove them and just let your eyes relax for a few minutes before opening them. If you open your eyes immediately after removing your fingers, you may find that they will not focus for several minutes. This is a normal result, and comes from the excellent relaxation that is induced by the exercise.

The yogis of the Far East, who studied these matters long before Bates or Babbitt, or even AMORC, believe that the two hands have different polarities of energy associated with them. The left side of the body is, they say, dominated by a feminine, or negative energy. The right side is positive and masculine.[20]

This was first noted centuries before our modern psychologists began to study the different functions of the left and right sides of the brain. Since then, it has been pointed out that the right hemisphere of the brain, which controls the left side of the body, is somehow connected with psychic phenomena. Itzhak Bentov has pointed out that *Kundalini* experiences usually manifest on the *left side* of the body.[21] And more than one authority has pointed out that *ectoplasm*, when it is seen 'oozing' from the body of a medium, always emerges from the *left side*.[22]

We are not going to produce any ectoplasm yet, though. We are going to make use of this phenomenon to extend vision in a different direction than Dr Bates. Having, I assumed, produced perfect vision in every one of my readers, I am going to now tell you how to extend vision beyond even that.

Since your right and left hands *do* have different polarities, when you bring them together, there tends to be a flow of energy from the one to the other. This produces an intensification of the *human aura* where the fingertips come together, and with practice, the aura can be made visible in a darkened room.

This effect was first noticed by an English physician named Walter John Kilner, who deserves credit as the first scientist to study the aura in a systematic manner. Dr Kilner used specially treated screens to make the aura visible, but I am going to ask you to do this experiment *without* a screen.

What you will need is a closet large enough to put a chair in, and two bath towels. Put your chair in your closet, close the door, and use your two towels to seal the crack under the door. This is necessary to prevent any light seeping in under the door. You should now be sitting in the closest thing to absolute darkness that you are likely to see in this lifetime.

Now bring your two hands together, palms touching, as if you were praying. Then, separate your palms, so that any energy that crosses over from one hand to the next must pass through your fingers. Kilner suggested that the fingers should be separated, so that the energy has to jump a short distance through space. But I have found that when the experiment is done in complete darkness, it is best to keep the fingers together.

Once you have positioned your hands, look at them and *will* that you be able to see the light that is being produced by the magnetic energy that is passing between them. After about ten minutes, stop. Then try again the next day.

You will not be able to see the light on the very first day, and you probably will not be able to see it on the second. Or the third. Or even the thirtieth. In fact, it may take you three or four months to begin getting results. But results you will surely get, if you merely persist.

The first results will be a faint glimmering that can be seen at some times and not at others. You should not be satisfied with this. It indicates that you are making progress, but you should persevere with this experiment until you can see a definite, steady, clear blue light where your fingertips join as soon as you enter your darkened room every time you enter. You will find that in doing this distributed practice is the key. In other words, five minutes a day every day of the week will produce more in the way of results than thirty-five minutes on Saturday afternoons.

You will also find that you are developing psychic sight. Many of the groups that teach this little experiment do not include with their directions what I feel are sufficient indications of the experiences their students are likely to have with it. Some of these experiences, while quite harmless, are likely to be rather disquieting if you are not prepared for them. And I want you to know that they are just the normal result of your newly extended vision.

One thing that you may see on occasion is a psychic projection. If you accept the possibility of projection, it should be obvious that there are people who are doing it, and that occasionally you may cross paths with one of them. I have looked up from something I was working on more than once to see a white figure glide right through the wall of my room, float soundlessly through the room itself, and vanish through the opposite wall. Usually these figures will be recognizably Oriental, for obvious reasons. They will also be quite oblivious to your presence. These little invasions of privacy happen all the time, but people cannot see them. After you have developed your psychic vision, you *will* see them.

You may also see lights of various kinds, usually when you are sitting in darkness meditating. They may be floating balls of light, or they may appear as if they were beamed from a powerful searchlamp. They may be coloured, and they may be pure white.

Opinion among Eastern mystics varies from one person to the next concerning these experiences. Generally, those who have seen these lights advise their students that to see them is proof of great spiritual development. Those who have *not* seen them seem to tend toward precisely the opposite viewpoint. Swami Muktananda even tried to categorize these experiences. He ranges them from a red light the size of the human body through white and black spots to a lentil-sized blue pearl.[23] The implication seems to be that if you have this kind of experience instead of that kind of experience, or that kind of experience instead of some other kind of experience, you are more or less advanced. I tend to suspect, though, that these lights suggest the presence of some kind of energy that is normally invisible, and that is apparent to people with trained sight. That you should see a red ball of light instead of a blue square of it merely indicates that energy conditions are this way instead of that. We can only read more meaning into these experiences if we assume that these conditions are of our own making.

In some cases these kinds of lights are produced deliberately as a form of communication. In *Old Diary Leaves*, Colonel Olcott relates an experience had by the medium W. Stainton Moses:

> I saw by my bedside, distant about two yards, and at the height of about 5′ 6″ from the floor, three small phosphorescent balls of light about the size of a small orange. They formed an equilateral triangle, the base of which would measure eighteen inches. I fixed my gaze on them and they remained quiet, glowing with a steady phosphorescent light which cast no gleam beyond itself. Satisfied that the phenomenon was objective, I reached for a match-box and struck a match. I could not see the balls through the matchlight; but when the match went out they came into view just as before. I repeated the match-striking six times (seven in all) when they paled and gradually went out.[24]

Olcott says that 'the three luminous spheres form the special symbol of the Lodge of our Adepts', meaning the Great White Lodge.[25]

If the fingertips-together experiment is not to your taste, you may accomplish the same thing by a certain *Sanyama* recommended by Patanjali. In Book three, *Sutra* forty-one, Patanjali says that 'by *Sanyama* on *Samana*, [there is produced] effulgence'.[26] This effulgence is merely an intensification of the human aura, just as we produced with the fingertips-together experiment. It results from the fact that the Solar Plexus area is the seat of the *Vayu* called *Samana*. *Samana* is the fire of digestion; however, the word 'fire' is to be taken literally as well as metaphorically. *Samana* not only digests your food; it is the seat of the *Tejas Tattwa* – the Fire Element – in the human body. By arousing and awakening this *Samana* through concentration, the yogi arouses and awakens the potencies of fire within himself. And those potencies include light.

They also include heat, and that is why I personally prefer the fingertips-together exercise. I find that my own concentration on *Samana* generates more heat than light. An uncomfortable *amount* of heat, in fact. Control of this particular *Vayu* is the basis of the yogic art of *tumo*, which enables naked ascetics in Tibet to take baths in freezing water.[27] Many Western critics of yoga believe that *tumo* is based on self-hypnosis, but, having done it myself, I am not so sure. The heat at least *feels* quite real, and if you do your experiments in a freezing apartment, you might prefer this method.

That said, let us take a look at how the experiment actually works. I have said that the lights you see are produced by energy in your surroundings. This energy is no way different from that which is called 'ball lightning' and which is known to science. But the light that is generated in these cases is outside the normal range of human vision. That is why only the Adepts can see it.

Light with a wavelength longer than about 700 millimicrons is invisible to virtually every human eye. It is in what we call the *infra-red* region, the 'redder than red' region. It is redder than the reddest red man can see, and it is therefore invisible.

The same thing is true with light that has a very short wavelength. These energies fall in what is called the *ultraviolet* region. Like infra-red rays, ultraviolet rays are beyond the normal range of human vision, and are therefore invisible.

The human aura is in this category. It consists of ultraviolet radiations. Since to normal people ultraviolet radiations are not visible, most people cannot see the aura. The range of the eyes can be extended, though, and this is in fact one of the trends of evolution. Says Richard Maurice Bucke:

Much more modern than the birth of the intellect was that of the colour sense. We have the authority of Max Müller for the statement that: 'It is well known that the distinction of colour is of late date: that Xenophanes knew of three colours of the rainbow only − purple, red, and yellow; that even Aristotle spoke of the tricoloured rainbow; and that Democritus knew of no more than four colours − black, white, red, and yellow.'

Geiger points out by examination of language that as late as fifteen or twenty thousand years ago man only perceived one colour. Pictet finds no names of colours in primitive Indo-European speech. And Max Müller finds no Sanskrit root whose meaning has any reference to colour.

At a later period red and black were recognized as distinct. Still later, when the Rig Veda was composed, red, yellow, and black were recognized as three separate shades, but these three included all the colour that man was capable of appreciating. Still later white was added to the list, and then green; but throughout the Rig Veda, the Zend Avesta, the Homeric poems, and the Bible the colour of the sky is not once mentioned; therefore, apparently, it was not recognized. For the omission can hardly be attributed to accident; the ten thousand lines of the Rig Veda are largely occupied with descriptions of the sky; and all its features − sun, moon, stars, clouds, lightnings, sunrise, and sunset − are mentioned hundreds of times. So also the Zend Avesta, to the writers of which light and fire, both terrestrial and heavenly, are sacred objects, could hardly have omitted by chance all mention of the blue sky. In the Bible, the sky and heaven are mentioned more than four hundred and thirty times, and still no mention is made of [their colour].

The English word blue and the German blau descend from a word that meant *black*. The Chinese *hi-u-an*, which now means sky-blue, formerly meant black. The world *nil*, which now in Persian and Arabic means blue, is derived from the name *Nile*, that is the *black river*, of which same word the Latin *Niger* is a form.[28]

The implication is obvious: that man's colour perception is gradually extending toward the blue-violet end of the colour spectrum. That means that man will eventually see auras. It is therefore not surprising that some people can already see them, and that the capability can be cultivated in others.

Now the reason all of us cannot see auras at the moment has more to do with accommodation than with the retina's spectral sensitivity. As Kilner explained it:

> The human eye is by no means a faultless optical instrument. It is imperfectly corrected for chromatic aberration, since the various colours come to a focus on different planes. The red being the least refrangible, [it] has its focus furthest from, and the violet nearest, the lens. The focus of the yellow is about midway between the yellow and the violet, and in the normal eye the yellow rays fall exactly on the retina, while the other colours come to a focus a little in front or behind it. Correction is arranged for in the brain centres.[29]

Ultraviolet rays come to a focus in front of the retina, whereas rays on the red side of yellow focus behind it. The brain can correct for a certain amount of defocusing, but as the colours come to a focus further and further away from the retina, they become less and less distinct. Finally, we arrive at the very edge of the visible spectrum. Colours beyond that point are invisible.

This is why observing the aura in a darkened room has the effect it does. There are no yellow rays in the room since you are sitting in complete datkness, and with a little effort, the eyes can be coaxed into focusing toward the more violet end of the spectrum. Red rays, which are normally visible, would in theory become invisible, and ultraviolet rays, which are normally invisible, would be moved into the visible range. Since the human aura is somewhere in the ultraviolet spectrum, the aura itself becomes visible.

This can be achieved to a limited degree in a lighted room by deliberately defocusing the eyes. In *How to Read the Aura*, W.E. Butler suggests that we do just that. 'This is done,' he said, 'by focusing them about six to nine inches beyond the subject.'[30] You will find that a delicate balance is needed here, which must be acquired by practice. There is a tendency to look directly at your subject, a habit which comes from a lifetime of experience, so that when you first begin to see the aura, you change your focus and it disappears. If this happens, merely shift your focus again, and the aura should come into view.

If you have any success with this, you will find that the aura's colours tend to shift with their owner's moods. We have all heard the expressions 'green with envy', 'yellow coward', 'seeing red', 'black mood of despair', and so on. These have to do with actual colours in the human aura, which seem to be produced by the corresponding emotions – a connection that was first noted by Plutarch in the first century. The black clouds that surround a depressed person are the easiest to see. Apparently, they are the closest of all the aura's colours to the spectrum of normally visible light. But others will become visible in time. One student of Transcendental Meditation who attained the state of Cosmic Consciousness, as understood by the Maharishi, reported that he 'would see energy surrounding people, little thin auras of different pastel colours, and bigger, egg-shaped ones, made out of huge spirals'.[31]

You may also discover the phenomenon that we might call *chromatic onomatopoeia* – the connection that apparently exists between colours and sounds. This connection becomes apparent for most people when under the influence of drugs. Baudelaire mentions it in *Paradis Artificiel* as one of the effects of smoking *hashish*. However, it comes to some occultists without recreational chemicals of any kind being involved. One begins to 'see' sounds and 'hear' colours. All of these are simply alterations in consciousness that may accompany the development of psychic sight.

Now as I said at the beginning of this chapter, some of these principles may be used in obscuring other people's sight as well as in extending your own. There is more that I could say about psychic sight, but I have already given you the specific principles that I referred to, and it is time now that we move on to the main topic of this book — the technique of invisibility itself.

6. How to Obscure Vision

Now that we know how to extend vision, let us consider how we are to obscure it. Not an easy thing to do, but it should be obvious that the best way for *us* to decide is to consider what others have decided in the past. That would seem to be a reasonable course of action. And in this *particular* case, 'others' means the medieval magicians – the authors of the *grimoires*.

The *grimoires* gives us some very strange advice, indeed. According to some of these, we should wear the heart of a bat, a black hen, or a frog under our right arms.[1] Albertus Magnus advises us to 'take the stone which is called *Ophthalmimis* and wrap it in the leaves of the laurel or bay tree. It is also called *Lapis Obthelmicus*, whose colour is not named, for it is of many colours, and of such virtue, that it blindeth the sight of those that stand about. Constantinus carrying this in his hand made himself invisible thereby.'[2]

The *Grimoirum Verum* suggests that we take the severed head of a suicide and bury it on a Wednesday morning before sunrise with seven black beans. The beans must be watered each morning thereafter with the very best brandy you have, until on the eighth morning, if you are successful, a spirit will appear. The spirit must be thoroughly tested, and if found true, allowed to water the head for you. The following morning, the beans will be seen to be sprouting, whereupon you must have a small girl pick and shell them for you. One of these beans will have the peculiar quality of making you invisible if you put it in your mouth.[3]

This experiment was actually tried at London in 1680 by two Jewish merchants, who used the garden of Mr Wyld Clark for the purpose. Procuring the severed head of a suicide is a bit of a bother even for a magician, and so the merchants made do with the head of a black cat, but in every other particular they observed the requirements of the *grimoire* with the greatest severity. They killed the cat under certain astrological aspects described in several versions of the grimoire, and severed the head and buried it with great ceremony, placing the magic beans in the cat's brain. When all was done, they awaited the morrow anxiously, then returned to the scene the following morning with a bottle of their very best booze. Alas for them, though! They had not buried the cat's head deeply enough. Their little experiment had attracted the attention of one of Mr Clark's roosters, who apparently was something of an occult student himself, and who dug up the head, thereby ruining all their Qabalistic symbols. 'They were crafty, subtile merchants,' wrote the source of the story, and yet 'they did believe it'.[4]

I am not sure that I do, and at any rate MacGregor Mathers, who is the high lord of modern occultism, at least in the Western Schools, has severely warned us against using the *Grimoirum Verum*. So let us proceed to another story that greatly intrigued the writers of medieval *grimoires* – the tradition of the Ring of Gyges.

Gyges was a king of Lydia, and the legendary ancestor of King Croesus – Croesus as in 'rich as Croesus'. He was in fact the founder of King Croesus' line, and was originally of humble birth, a man who used the power of invisibility to acquire his kingdom.

According to Plato, Gyges was a shepherd who was tending his flocks one day when a great storm suddenly arose, accompanied by an earthquake, which rent the earth asunder in the area where he was sitting. He was astonished at this, and proceeded to the crevasse, where he discovered, among other things, a hollow brazen horse, with doors mounted on the sides. He managed to force the doors open, and found the body of a man inside, a man of more than mortal stature, who was completely nude, save for a golden ring, which Gyges naturally appropriated for his own use.

Later, when Gyges was at a meeting of the shepherds, held that they might prepare a monthly report for the king on the state of their flocks, he was wearing the golden ring, and he chanced to turn it in such a way that its collet was inside his hand. Immediately, he became invisible to the rest of the company, and they began to speak of him as if he were no longer present. He was astonished at this, and by experimenting with the ring, found that in this manner he could make himself visible or invisible at will. He then contrived to get on the committee that was to go to the palace, and once there, used his power of invisibility to make his way to the chambers of the queen. He made love to the queen, and when he was through, she evidently decided that he would make a better king than the fellow she had married. Together, they plotted against the king's life, killed him, and seized the kingdom.[5]

Of course, that was the only form of social mobility there was in those days, and one can hardly blame Gyges for trying to better his lot; but to Plato, the moral of the story was clear: the invisible man is not to be trusted.

'Suppose,' he wrote, 'that there were two such magic rings, and the just [man] put on one of them and the unjust the other. No man can be imagined to be of such an iron nature that he would stand fast in justice. No man would keep his hands off what was not his own when he could safely take what he liked out of the market, or go into houses and lie with anyone at his pleasure, or kill or release from prison whom he would, and in all respects be like a god among men. If you could imagine anyone obtaining this power of becoming invisible, and never doing any wrong or touching what was another's, he would be thought by the lookers-on to be a most wretched idiot, although they would praise him to one another's faces, and keep up appearances with one another from a fear that they, too, might suffer in injustice.'[6]

Plato's view was based on his theory that, in his words, 'to *do* injustice is, by nature, good; to *suffer* injustice, evil.'[7] However, I do not believe most modern men would agree with him, and for those who believe in divine justice, there is always the possibility that Reginald Scot pointed out, to wit: 'that God doth see both them and their knavery'.[8] Nonetheless, invisibility does present an ethical problem, and all the magic manuals deal with the ethics before they disclose the techniques.

A Chinese alchemist warned that these techniques 'are not to be used heedlessly, such as for example to produce outbursts of amazement when employed without reason in company. They may be used only in dire necessity against military reversals and dangerous crises, for in that way no harm will be incurred.'[9] The Arabs have a similar belief: invisibility is permissible in case of a reversal on the battlefield, when it is necessary to stay alive, and for that purpose they employ the *cat's eye*.[10] Even Abraham the Jew, who does not shrink from invoking the evil spirits, says that although 'to render oneself invisible is a very easy matter, it is not altogether permissible, because by such a means we can annoy our neighbour in his daily life ... and we can also work an infinitude of evils.'[11]

More modern students, however, doubt that such admonitions are really necessary. Anyone who would wish to employ the power of invisibility for an evil purpose will for that reason be prevented from getting it. He will lack the requisite degree of spirituality.

In illustration of this point, permit me another story. On 18 March, 1582, two Spaniards decided to emulate the example of Gyges the Lydian and try to kill the Prince of Orange, and to that end proposed to work the experiment of invisibility. The method they used supposedly would make only one person invisible at a time, and since it worked only on the human body, it was necessary for him to remove all his clothing. Now it is traditional for one experimenting with invisibility to use a mirror, and to employ it at the critical time to see if the experiment has been or still is a success. That the foolish Spaniard failed to do, and when he made it to the palace of the Prince, he was not only completely visible, but completely naked as well. The palace guard let the odd visitor pass as if they did not see him, but kept him under observation until it became clear that his intention was to do harm to the Prince. The Prince naturally took umbrage at this, and ordered the poor Spaniard soundly flogged.[12]

According to one source, the Ring of Gyges should be made of fixed mercury, and set with a small stone to be found in the lapwing's nest. Around the stone, one must engrave the words '*Jesus passant par le milieu d'eux s'en allait*'. Put this on your finger – so say the *grimoires* – and you will be invisible.[13]

However, the maker should know that this formula is not to be taken literally. Fixed mercury is an alchemical term, and undoubtedly refers to the Mercury of the Wise, which we have already identified with the First Matter − the material of the *cloud*. A ring, of course, surrounds some part of the body, in this case the finger, but if we interpret it loosely, we could say that it surrounds the entire body.

As for the stone to be found in the lapwing's nest, Albertus Magnus informs us that it is called Quiritia.[14] This has been identified with the aforementioned Opthalmimis.[15] The French text that is to be 'engraved' around the stone (how does one engrave a text on the *cloud*?) refers to an incident in the Bible in which Jesus is supposed to have made himself invisible and walked among the Pharisees.[16]

'We will not repeat here the mystifications of the vulgar *grimoires* concerning the ring of invisibility,' wrote Eliphas Lévi. 'One composes it of fixed mercury and would that we guard it in a box of the same metal, after having set it with a small stone which must be found in the nest of a lapwing.* The author of the *Petit Albert* would that one make this ring with hairs torn from the head of an infuriated hyena; it is similar to the history of the bell of Rodilard. The only authors who have spoken seriously of the Ring of Gyges are Iamblichus, Porphyry, and Pierre d'Apono.'

That which they say is evidently allegorical, and the figure that they give, or that one might make based on their description, proves that by the Ring of Gyges they intend no other thing than the Great Magical Arcanum.

One of these figures represents the cycle of universal movement, harmonic and equilibrated in imperishable being; the other, which should be made from an amalgam of the seven metals, merits a particular description.

It should have a double collet and two precious stones, a topaz constellated in the sign of the Sun, and an emerald in the sign of the

---

* The French word for lapwing is *huppe*, and Eliphas Lévi says that 'au lieu de *huppe*, c'est *dupe* qu'il faudrait lire', a statement that requires no translation. I am inclined to favour my own interpretation.

Moon; interiorly, it should show the occult characters of the planets, and exteriorly their known signs, repeated twice in Qabalistic opposition, one to the other, that is to say, five on the right and five on the left, the signs of the Sun and Moon resuming the four diverse intelligences of the seven planets. This configuration is nothing but a pentacle expressing all the mysteries of magical dogma, and the symbolic sense of the ring is, that to exert the total power of which ocular fascination is one of the most difficult proofs to give, one must possess the whole science and knowledge of its usage.

Fascination operates by magnetism. The magician ordains interiorly to an entire assembly that they will not see him, and they do not. He enters thus past guarded portals; he leaves prisons before stupefied gaolers. One feels a strange numbness, and remembers having seen the magician as if in a dream, but only after he has gone. The secret of invisibility is therefore entirely in a power that one may define: that of turning or paralyzing the attention, so that light arrives at the visual organ without exciting the regard of the soul.

To exercise this power, one must have a will habituated to acts both energetic and sudden, a great presence of spirit, and a no less great skill at causing distractions in the crowd.[17]

There is little doubt that this feat can be performed by advanced occultists. In his *Old Diary Leaves*, Colonel Olcott ascribes this ability to the celebrated Coptic magician, Paulos Metamon, who was one of the mentors of Madame Blavatsky. He says:

From an eye-witness I had it that while H.P.B. was in Cairo the most extraordinary phenomena would occur in any room she might be sitting in; for example, the table lamp would quit its place on one table and pass through the air to another, just as if carried in some one's hand; this same mysterious Copt would suddenly vanish from the sofa where he was sitting, and many such marvels. Miracles no longer, since we have had the scientists prove to us the possibility of inhibition of the senses of sight, hearing, touch and smell by mere hypnotic suggestion. Undoubtedly this inhibition was provoked in

the company present, who were made to see the Copt vanish, and
the lamp moving through space, but not the person whose hand was
carrying it. It was what H.P.B. called a 'psychological trick', yet all
the same a fact and one of moment to science.[18]

It appears that Madame Blavatsky herself performed this experiment on
occasion, no doubt following Paulos Metamon's instructions. One of
these occasions took place when she and the colonel were staying in
Philadelphia. As the colonel describes it:

Her house in Philadelphia was built on the local plan, with a front
building and a wing at the back which contained the dining-room
below and sitting or bedrooms above. H.P.B.'s bedroom was the
front one on the first floor of the main building; at the turn of the
staircase was the sitting-room, and from its open door one could
look straight along the passage into H.P.B.'s room if her door also
stood open. She had been sitting in the former apartment conversing
with me, but left to get something from her bedroom. I saw her
mount the few steps to her floor, enter her room, and leave the door
open. Time passed, but she did not return. I waited and waited,
until, fearing that she might have fainted, I called her name. There
was no reply, so now, being a little anxious, and knowing that she
could not be engaged privately, since the door had not been closed,
I went there, called again, and looked in; she was not visible,
though I even opened the closet and looked under the bed. She had
vanished, without the chance of having walked out in the normal
way, for, save the door giving upon the landing, there was no
other means of exit; the room was a *cul de sac*. I was a cool one
about phenomena after my long course of experiences, but this
puzzled and worried me. I went back to the sitting room, lit a pipe,
and tried to puzzle out the mystery. This was in 1875, many years
before the Salpetriere school's experiments in hypnotism had been
vulgarised, so it never occurred to me that I was the subject of a neat
experiment in mental suggestion, and that H.P.B. had simply
inhibited my organs of sight from perceiving her presence, perhaps
within two paces of me in the room. After a while she calmly came

out of her room into the passage and returned to the sitting room to
me. When I asked where she had been, she laughed and said she had
some occult business to attend to, and had made herself invisible.
But how, she would not explain. She played me and others the same
trick at other times, before and after our going to India.[19]

Scientists attest the fact of inhibition yet confess ignorance as to its
rationale. 'How,' say Drs Binet and Fere in their celebrated work *Le
Magnetisme Animal*, 'has the experimentalist produced this curious
phenomenon? We know nothing about it. We only grasp the
external fact, to know that when one affirms to a sensitive subject
that an object present does not exist, this suggestion has the effect,
direct or indirect, to dig in the brain of the hypnotis an anesthesia
corresponding to the designated object. But what happens between
the verbal affirmation, which is the means, and the systematized
anesthesia, which is the end? ... Here the laws of association, which
are so great a help in solving psychological problems, abandon us
completely.' Poor beginners! They do not see that the inhibition is
upon the astral man, and Eastern magicians excel them in
psychological tricks simply because they know more about
psychology, and can reach the Watcher who peers out upon the
foolish world of illusion through the windows of the body; the
telephonic nerves being inhibited, the telegraphic nerves are cut,
and no message passes in.[20]

The superior neatness of Oriental over Western hypnotic suggestion
is that in such cases as this, the inhibitory effect upon the person's
perceptive organs *results from mental, not spoken, command or suggestion.*
The subject is not put on his guard to resist the illusion, and it is
done before he had the least suspicion that any experiment is being
made at his expense.[21]

Now this is a very common interpretation of the experiment of
invisibility, and was discussed at length by certain ancient writers,
including Alexander of Hales, who concluded that these performances
were the result of a delusion of the senses, rather than any change in the

material world itself.[22] In ancient times these illusions were called *glamours*, or *prestiges*, from the word *prestringo*, 'since the sight of the eyes is so fettered that things seem to be other than what they are'.[23] Modern scientists call them *negative hallucinations*.

A negative hallucination is just the opposite of a positive one. Whereas in positive hallucination one sees something that is not there, in negative hallucination one fails to see something that is there. Actually, the two are quite closely related. As one modern authority pointed out:

> [Negative hallucination] poses something of a problem, because in order *not* to see Mr X at different places in the room, [the hypnotized subject] must *see* Mr X ... Subjective reports of individuals with such a negative hallucination indicate they experience either the presence in the room of something 'peculiar' with a 'not-to-be-inquired-into' aspect, or the existence of a white space for Mr X. This peculiarity is more interesting to the viewer than to the subject, who appears to find no incongruity in the situation.[24]

As Forel explains:

> We cannot see a gap in the visual field without filling it in with something, be it only a black background. Conversely, we cannot be affected with a positive hallucination unless a portion of the visual field is covered with the hallucinatory object. If the appropriate portion of the real background be not absolutely blocked out by the hallucinatory object, it is at least rendered hazy, as happens in the case of transparent hallucinations. The same thing occurs in the case of many hallucinations of hearing and of tactile sensation ... One who, when lying in bed, has the hallucination that he is lying on a pin cushion, can no longer feel the soft mattress.[25]

A negative hallucination can therefore be considered a special form of positive hallucination, in which one hallucinates a white or black space to cover whatever one is not to see. Since the hallucinating person.

is in a special sense aware of the presence of the person of whose presence he is not to be aware, that leads to some curious phenomena.

'If the subject's hallucination denies the presence of a seated observer,' observes H.L. Shaw, 'the subject will find some undefined reason for avoiding the chair.'[26] This is contrary to what most people think i.e., that the hallucinating person will unintentionally sit in the invisible man's lap, and involves what is technically known as 'trance logic'.

Trance logic is, quite simply, illogical. Things which are manifestly illogical to an impartial observer are seen as quite logical to a hypnotized person if that is what he must believe to maintain the integrity of his belief system. Therefore, if he believes that Mr X has left the room, even though Mr X is obviously present, he will accept whatever illogical notions he must accept to continue denying Mr X's presence.

This seems so very odd to most people that many laymen are inclined to doubt the reality of hypnosis. But real it certainly is, and in fact trance logic is quite common, even in people who are *not* hypnotized.

Almost anyone who holds a strong conviction about something will show signs of trance logic if he is confronted with evidence that belies his beliefs. I saw a television programme once in Los Angeles in which a man was featured whose mission in life was to convince people that the earth is flat. The programme presenter's role was to stimulate discussion on that topic, and to do that he confronted his guest with a photograph of the earth that had been taken from several thousand miles in space. The flat-earth spokesman acknowledged that the photograph was genuine, that it was indeed a photograph of the earth, and that in fact the earth appeared to be round. That was no problem, though, he explained, because *anything* looked at from a great distance looks round. 'You mean that if you looked at me from a distance, I would appear to be round?' the presenter asked. 'Yes, sir,' was the answer.

In one of his books, Binet quotes an astonishing account of an experiment with negative hallucination that was performed by Bernheim and Liegeois, which serves to further illuminate this extraordinary phenomenon. The subject was an eighteen-year-old servant girl named Elsie B. The hypnotist put her into a deep trance, and then told her: 'When you awaken you will no longer see me. I shall have gone.' She woke, and, just as the hypnotist had suggested, she did not notice his presence. However, she did more than just that. She looked about for him, but did not notice him, even though he was sitting directly in front of her. If he shouted at her, she did not hear. If he penetrated her skin with pins, she did not feel. 'As far as she was concerned, I had ceased to exist,' he wrote, 'and all the acoustic, visual, tactile, and other impressions emanating from myself did not make the slightest impression upon her; she ignored them all ... Wishing to see, on account of its medico-legal bearing, whether a serious offence might be committed under cover of a negative hallucination, I roughly raised her dress and skirt. Although naturally very modest, she allowed this without a blush.'[27] A moment later, though, she was blushing a very great deal. The hypnotist suggested to her that she would 'remember' the incidents that, a moment before, she did not even seem to be aware of. She did remember, yet she was altogether unable to believe that she had allowed herself to be exposed, and, when queried, reported that she remembered the incident *as if it took place in a dream*.

This is exactly the experience that Eliphas Lévi described – the Magus will be remembered by the stupefied gaolers, but as if in a dream – and that suggests that Eliphas Lévi might have known of actual incidents in which this power was used. It also suggests an interesting theory about how the negative hallucinations take place.

M. Liegeois believed that the hypnotized person really did 'see' him, but that her personality was for the moment split into two parts. There was the conscious aspect of her which was unable to see that he was in the room, and there was an unconscious, second ego, that was quite aware of his existence, but which had been forbidden by the hypnotist to inform the conscious part. One would expect that these two parts of the person's mind could 'get together' at a later date and produce a dream-like memory of the experience, but by then the purpose of the exercise – whatever it might have been – would have been achieved.

I might point out here that sight is one of the most easily affected conscious functions by hypnosis. In ancient times it was common for people to be 'struck blind', that is, to suddenly go blind without any damage to the eyes, purely because of suggestion. Some rationalist historians even believe that that is the basis for ancient miracle stories about the blind being made suddenly to see. Today, this phenomenon is called 'hysteria', or 'conversion neurosis', but it is not so common as before,, not because suggestion has ceased to operate, but because people no longer believe in being struck blind. Faith is the essential factor in the disease, and faith is also the essential factor in the cure.

There are some formulas and techniques in ancient magical papyri, especially Egyptian texts like the Leiden papyrus, for striking a person blind, but I shall not give them here because unlike the experiment of invisibility, which is a highly selective and temporary thing, striking someone blind seems to me to be an extremely vicious form of magic. It is worth mentioning, though, that this kind of spell is quite easily reversed, provided the victim can summon the same kind of faith in his prospect for a cure that produced his blindness in the first place.

All the ancient stories of the blind being cured are remarkably similar, and I give here an incident that shows that one need not be a sage or a saint or produce a cure. The following incident concerns the Roman Emperor Vespasian, and is given us by Tacitus:

Vespasian passed some months at Alexandria, having resolved to defer his voyage to Italy till the return of summer, when the winds, blowing in a regular direction, afford a safe and pleasant navigation. During his residence in that city, a number of incidents, out of the ordinary course of nature, seemed to mark him as a peculiar favourite of the gods. A man of mean condition, born at Alexandria, had lost his sight by a defluxion on his eyes. He presented himself before Vespasian, and, falling prostrate on the ground, implored the emperor to administer a cure for his blindness. He came, he said, by the admonition of Serapis, a god for whom the Egyptians have the highest veneration. The request was that the emperor, with his spittle, would condescend to moisten the poor man's face and the balls of his eyes. Another, who had lost the use of his hand, inspired by the same god, begged that he would tread on the part affected ... In the presence of a prodigious multitude, all erect with expectation, he advanced with an air of serenity, and hazarded the experiment. The paralytic hand recovered its functions, and the blind man saw the light of the sun. By living witnesses, who were actually on the spot, both events are confirmed at this hour, when deceit and flattery can hope for no reward.[28]

Doane, who was rather sceptical of such matters, points out that identical stories are told of Jesus. In the Gospel according to Mark we read: 'And he cometh to Bethsaida, and they bring a blind man unto him, and besought him to touch him. And he took the blind man by the hand ... and when he had spat on his eyes ... he looked up and said: 'I see men and trees' ... and he was restored.'[29]

There is some evidence, though, that human spittle may have some curative properties. In ancient Egyptian mythology there is a story that the god Thoth cured the eye of Horus with spittle, and we can surely not believe that the ancient Egyptians copied it from Tacitus.[30] It is rather more likely that conversion neuroses were common in those days, and that the stories show how easy it is for a highly skilled faith healer to correct them. In any event, the point is proved: the mind has temendous power over the eye.

In *The Way Out World* Long John Nebel quotes a story that sounds like a case of suggested invisibility. The invisible man was stage magician William Neff. Describing what he saw, Long John says: 'I felt that [Neff's] clothed body was turning to frosted glass or some form of plastic that was not transparent, but would permit light areas to be seen through it ... As the seconds ticked away ... the body was now undergoing a complete change. It now appeared that it was no longer translucent, but completely transparent ... [Then], slowly, it was no longer transparent; it was disappearing completely.'[31]

Asked about the incident later, Mr Neff denied that the effect was produced by illusion, or even that he was aware that it was happening. Moreover, he told Nebel about an incident in which he apparently became invisible to his own wife, again spontaneously, and again without any conscious trickery on his part.[32] I can only conclude that this must have been the result of suggestion, and, that being the case, it behoves us as students of *practical* invisibility to take a look at hypnotic techniques.

Hypnotism seems to be the basis of invisibility experiments in such *grimoires* as the *Key of Solomon*, although of course the name hypnotism had yet to be coined.

Solomon categorizes 'operations of mockery, invisibility, and deceit' together, and suggests an evocation directed toward all the spirits who 'love the times and places wherein all kinds of mockeries and deceits are practised'.[33] One part of the evocation is particularly suggestive:

> And ye who make things disappear and render them invisible, come hither to *deceive* all those who regard these things, so that they may be *deceived*, and that they may seem to see that which they see not, and hear that which they hear not, so that their senses may be *deceived*, and that they behold that which is not true.[34]

MacGregor Mathers, who translated the *Key to Solomon*, incorporated portions of this evocation in the 'Ritual of Invisibility' that he passed around privately to members of his Hermetic Order of the Golden Dawn.[35] Thus we find statements in the G.D. manuscripts such as this: 'Seeing me, men may see me *not*, neither understand. But that they may see the thing that they see not, and comprehend not the thing that they behold.'[36] This prompted a writer in *Man, Myth and Magic* to write that 'the ritual is not intended to make the operator *literally* invisible, but to allow him to pass unnoticed, inscrutable.'[37] Actually, that is not accurate; the G.D. ritual aimed at objective invisibility as well, but did use methods aimed at mass hypnosis. The *Key to Solomon*, though, used the techniques of ceremonial magic. Oriental magicians use techniques more familiar to students of modern hypnotism.

There is a good deal of speculation among Western students as to just how the Orientals really do produce their effects. Some authorities believe that rhythmic swaying and chanting has a hypnotic effect on the minds of a fakir's audience. Theodore Flournoy speculates that the hot tropical sun and the use of 'powerful fumigants' also contribute.[38] But according to one of the modern practitioners of the Oriental methods, a man who studied in both India and Mathraw, Persia, the method is truly telepathic.

The hypnotist in question is Dr J.D. Ward, who wrote an

extraordinary article for *The Rosicrucian Digest* on 'Suspended Animation' in 1931.[39] This article is the only one I have ever seen in which the stages of suspended animation are described in detail, and in which actual experiences of a soul liberated by this amazing process are also recounted. Dr Ward also tells the secret of Oriental hypnotism via telepathy: it is to 'shout' your hypnotic commands at your subject mentally.

Using this method, Dr Ward claims to have stopped the pulse in a man's arm in a demonstration at Dallas, Texas, in 1899. This mental shouting technique is used in the early stages of inducing suspended animation at certain Indian monasteries, according to Dr Ward, and is quite effective.

Another authority, Dr Leon H. Zeller, also advocates the use of mentally induced suggestion, although he warns that, although 'it is often done', yet 'it will not succeed in so great a number of cases'.[40] Dr Zeller suggests training the will first, by concentrating on a disk of white paper, about the size of the end of a pencil, that should be afixed to the surface of a mirror.[41] Even the Russians are working on this, and publish a journal, entitled *Suggestion At A Distance*, which 'attempts on an empirical basis to deal with this phenomenon under relatively controlled circumstances.'[42]

Hypnotist Harry Arons has performed this feat numerous times with large groups and in front of an audience. Mr Arons will ask for volunteers from his audience, specifically calling for people who are difficult to hypnotize. Then, when they arrive on stage, he tells them that he will put them in a trance within one minute, *without using any spoken suggestions whatsoever.* An impartial third party is asked to keep the time, and, one minute later, most of his subjects are indeed hypnotized. 'I have rarely had less than 80 per cent success,' he says.[43]

The remarkable thing, though, is that Mr Arons not only does not use spoken suggestions; he does not even use mental suggestions. Because unlike Dr Ward and some of the others, Arons knows that his technique is not really telepathic. It only *seems* to be.

The important thing is to carefully instruct the subjects before the mental suggestions are administered what you are going to do. Then, when you observe your period of silence and direct your thoughts at them, they will think they are responding to telepathic commands, whereas in fact they are responding to your preliminary instructions. The suggestions really are spoken, but they are given in a sneaky fashion, so that the subjects do not recognize them for what they are.

For example, let us take Dr Ward's experiment: stopping the pulse in a man's arm by 'shouting' the command mentally. Suppose that before the demonstration, Dr Ward explained very carefully to his subject that the pulse in his arm was going to stop, and that the suggestions that would bring this about would be mental, unspoken. When Dr Ward then closed his eyes, perhaps furrowed his brow, and started shouting his commands mentally, the subject would then believe that he was being affected by the mental suggestions. But the real suggestions *would already have been given.*

Furthermore, although it is no doubt true that the advanced Yoga masters of the Far East possess the power to hypnotize people at will, it is rather less likely that ordinary conjurers employ these techniques, and it is they who put on the shows that travellers come back and tell about. Hereward Carrington, who wrote a book about Indian magic tricks entitled *Hindu Magic*, says that 'personally, I doubt whether hallucinations ... play any part at all at these performances.'

> I am inclined, on the contrary, to believe that they are all the result of trickery. I made a careful search for the evidence bearing on this question of hallucination in their performances when writing *The Psychic Phenomena of Spiritualism*, and came to the deliberate conclusion that there was practically no first-hand evidence that such hallucinations existed ... I have had no reason to change my belief since the above was written.[44]

And finally, where hypnotically-induced invisibility is concerned, there is the difficulty of achieving the necessary state of trance. On the Davis and Husband Scale, negative hallucination is given a 30, which marks it as one characteristic of a somnambulist, and the most profound indicator of deep hypnotic trance.[45] Only a few people out of every hundred are capable of entering such a profound trance, which is why hypnotically induced invisibility had never been demonstrated before a large group. Only small audiences of one or two persons have ever seen it done.

We must not abandon our interest in hypnotism altogether, however, because we are faced with a curious paradox, to wit: whereas hypnotic *suggestions* cannot be used to produce the phenomenon of invisibility, *the hypnotic eye can.*

7. Forming the Cloud

'Look into my eyes.' If you are old enough to remember the bad movies that used to be made about hypnotism in the 1950s, you will surely recognize that phrase. In most of these films the hypnotist – who was usually the villain – was shown with great, bulging eyes that could make fair maidens lose their clothing and respectable young men commit horrid crimes. The eyes were often exaggerated to emphasize the point that it was from these remarkable organs that the hypnotist acquired his power over others. When he was finally vanquished, the hero had to avoid gazing into his eyes, lest he, too, become a mere pawn in the hypnotist's sinister game.

In the last twenty years or so there has been a movement to transform hypnotism from an occult science into a 'respectable' science – an artificial distinction if there ever was one – and in the process the use of the eyes has been de-emphasized. Modern hypnotism depends more on the spoken suggestion that on the hypnotic gaze, but the power of the eye is still there to be cultivated, for good or for evil..

Every child knows that the eye can be used to dominate another person. A person with weak will has difficulty maintaining eye-contact with other people, and it is common belief, if not fact, that a liar will betray himself if he looks into the eye of his victim.

It is for this reason that the 'shifty-eyed' person is mistrusted. Professionals who deal with other people in their business make a practice of maintaining eye-contact with their clients deliberately, avoiding domination by focusing on the root of the other man's nose.

In some cases, the power of the eye can almost be felt as a physical force. When Japanese diplomat Toshikazu Kase boarded the American warship *Missouri* at the end of the Second World War to formalize his country's surrender to the allies, 'A million eyes seemed to beat on us with the million shafts of a rattling storm of arrows barbed with fire. I felt their keenness sink into my body with a sharp physical pain. Never have I realized that the glance of glaring eyes could hurt so much.'[1] It was a case of a single shattered will being beaten down by a thousand stronger ones.

It is also well known that certain animals have this power and use it in catching their prey, notably cats and snakes. As Edmund Shaftesbury describes it:

> The cat closes its iris to a vertical line when it is out in the sun; but let a bird come near by and the iris will instantly give way, allowing the pupil to expand so as to cover the whole area, even in the brightest glare of sunlight ... The bird suffers nothing in the jaws of the cat. Something in the expanded pupils and glaring balls of the captor has lessened the will of the prey, and the sensation of drowsiness that follows may deaden the feeling in the nerves.[2]

This performance is similar to hypnotism in its effects and works not only on lower animals, but on humans as well. I was almost hypnotized this way once by my own cat.

He was a Russian Blue, a breed noted for its exceptional intelligence. He caught me staring vacantly into space one day, jumped up on the table in front of me, and proceeded to try the expanded-pupil trick. It was quite effective. My mind was wandering who-knows-where, when suddenly I had the most extraordinary feeling come over me, as if someone were trying to dominate me by some psychic means. Like all humans, I am possessed with the absurd conceit that ours is the 'superior' species, and was able to shake off the feeling with a simple act of will, only to realize that I had been hypnotized by my own pet.

The influence works the other way as well. The best way of stopping a charging dog is to stand quietly and look the animal straight in the eye. Dogs are more humble than cats are — at least where humans are concerned — and will not attack until they have elicited a clear sign of submission from their victim.

It was also once believed that camels could be forced into a ditch by the mere glance of an enchanter — an opinion which the University of Paris found it necessary to formally condemn.[3] It might be thought that all this is merely psychological, but Sprenger, who has this story, says that 'that influence which is exerted over another often proceeds from the eyes, *for in the eyes a certain subtle influence may be concentrated.*'[4]

Madame Blavatsky would agree. In *Isis Unveiled* she says that fakirs in India can effect magical cures 'by merely pronouncing certain magical words', but 'if a strong mesmeric fluid — say *projected from the eye*, and without any other contact — is not added, no magical words would be efficacious'.[5]

You can easily test this contention for yourself if you wish. You will need another person for the experiment, preferably someone whose age is within ten years of yours. Sit facing the other person and stare directly into his eyes while he stares directly into yours, and keep in mind that you are going to force your partner to look away, while he of course does the same thing to you. No threatening faces are necessary, and no verbal or physical threats are to be given. Each of you is merely to stare quietly into the other's eyes. The attempts at dominance are to be kept purely at the mental, telepathic, level.

If you do this correctly, you should begin to feel the force emanating from your partner's eyes within a few seconds. Whereas you would not have the slightest difficulty staring at his nose or chin, or hair, his eyes will seem to project a power that makes it difficult to keep looking. After a few moments, both of you will be struggling to continue the contest, and within a minute you should know which of you has the stronger personality.

The ancients took it for granted that this was caused by an actual energy, and they based some of their early theories of vision on it. As Plato wrote in the *Timaeus*: 'So much of Fire as would not burn, but gave a gentle light, [the gods] formed into a substance akin to the light of everyday life, and the pure Fire which is within us and related thereto they made to *flow through the eyes* in a stream smooth and dense ...'[6] Plato thought that this energy was necessary to vision and that 'when the light of day surrounds the stream of vision [from the eyes], like falls upon like', producing sight 'wherever the light that falls from within meets with an external object'.[7]

Empedocles believed much the same thing. As Zeller interprets his theories, 'the seeing body was supposed to issue forth from the eye in order to come into contact with the emanations of the object'.

> Empedocles thus conceived the eye as a kind of lantern; in the apple of the eye Fire and Water are enclosed in skins, the pores of which, arranged in alternate rows for each substance, allow passage to the emanations of each; Fire causes the perception of that which is bright and Water of that which is dark. When, therefore, emanations of visible things reach the eye, the emanations of the internal Fire and Water pass out of the eye through the pores, and from the meeting of the two arises vision.[8]

He thought that Fire predominated in blue-eyed people, whereas Water predominated in brown eyes. In this manner he explained the well known fact that blue-eyed people tend to myopia, whereas brown-eyed people are more inclined to night blindness. The Fire Element was weaker in the eyes of the brown-eyed folks, and that Element was essential in night vision.[9]

Aristotle was not quite so sure. He divided the theories of seeing into two categories: those which held that sight 'issues forth', and those which depended on 'movement derived from the visible object'.[10] However, after carefully examining both theories, he concluded that 'it is unreasonable to suppose that seeing occurs by something issuing from the eye.'[11]

That something does issue from the eye, though, he readily admitted, and in his little essay *On Dreams*, he refers to the well-known fact that a menstruating woman can produce a light mist on the surface of a mirror, merely by staring at it. 'When menstruation takes place, the difference of condition in the eyes, though invisible to us, is nonetheless real, and the eyes set up a movement in the air. This imparts a certain quality to the layer of air extending itself over the mirror, and this layer affects the surface of the mirror.'[12]

Even though he was not willing to allow this energy any place in the explanation of vision, Aristotle readily admitted that it existed, and that 'the organ of sight is not only acted upon by its object, but acts upon it' as well.[13] So far all parties agree: the light from the eyes does exist.

Now I may as well point out here that the mirrors that were in use in Aristotle's time are not the same as the mirrors we use today. Ancient Greek mirrors were made of highly polished brass. The surface of the metal was 'silvered' with arsenic, antimony, or mercury, all of which require special skills to handle safely, and the finished product was lightly waxed to insure the quality of the reflective surface.[14]

There are easier ways of proving the existence of this energy. The AMORC Rosicrucians have an experiment that they sometimes perform in their Lodges in which the energy from the eyes becomes visible in a darkened room. Shaftesbury refers to observations that Daniel Webster and Rufus Choate – both powerful orators – had eyes that 'glowed' like burning coals.[15] He himself claimed to have 'witnessed lines of fire proceeding far into the room' whenever one of his students deliberately tried to intensify the light from his eyes.[16]

Centuries ago, occultists called upon this energy from the eyes to explain glamours and prestiges. In his *Philosophy of Natural Magic,* Cornelius Agrippa explains that there is a 'vapour' that emanates from the eyes. Marcus Fienus, a Florentine physician, uses almost the same language. He says that 'a vapour, or a certain spirit' is 'emitted by the rays of the eyes'.[17] In more modern times, we call this 'vapour' the *cloud.*

This is why Morien tells King Khalid that the First Matter 'is firmly captive within you yourself, inseparable from you wherever you may be … [It] comes from you, who are yourself its source, where it is found and whence it is taken.'[18] It is in theory possible to 'dissolve' common elements into the First Matter, but in practice, the substance is produced directly from the emanations of the human body. Likewise, Hermes says that 'the Work is both within you and without you; taking what is within and fixed, thou canst have it either in earth or in sea.'[19]

That said, it is now time for me to stop throwing theories at you and tell you precisely how you are to form the cloud, either for materialization or for invisibility. Every principle that we shall use has been given to you already. What remains is to draw the loose ends together into a definite technique.

All told, there are *seven steps* – a number that will ring a bell with students of alchemy. We shall consider each of the seven in turn.

STEP ONE

The first step is to construct your laboratory. Every alchemist has to have a laboratory, and modern alchemists are no exception. But your laboratory does not have to look like something that might be owned by the Dow Chemical Corporation. Al-chemical laboratories can be quite simple. In fact, you will need no conventional chemical apparatus at all.

'What shall I say to you,' asked Paracelsus, 'about all your alchemical prescriptions, about all your retorts and bottles, crucibles, mortars, and glasses, of all your complicated processes of distilling, melting, cohibiting, coagulating, sublimating, precipitating, and filtering, of all the tomfoolery for which you throw away your time and money. All such things are useless and the labour for it is lost. They are rather an impediment than a help to arrive at the truth.'[20] The true ancestors of the chemists were not the alchemists, but their despised brethren, the puffers – also known as broilers, souffleurs, and cacochemists. Unless you are a chemist, you may leave the glassware and the bunsen burners to them. They are of no use to you in alchemy.

There are of course some chemical facts that you may wish to take into consideration. In *Psychic Self Defence* Dion Fortune gives some advice for *preventing* materializations, say, by an enemy. She suggests 'consecrated salt', dissolved in vinegar and placed in saucers, for 'low degrees of force', and nitric acid, either diluted or full strength, for higher degrees.[21] Obviously, in this case, we are trying for just the opposite, so if you have any consecrated salt about, you might wish to exclude it from your laboratory. The same goes for nitric acid.

Other than that, the problem of setting up your laboratory is mostly one of atmosphere. The Spiritualists, who have experimented more with materialization than anyone else, claim that light is detrimental to 'physical' phenomena. Best to try it in darkness. I do not happen to believe that one should go *that* far, but you will find it desirable to have a room where you can limit the amount of outside light. Just the amount of light that usually is seen at late twilight seems to be best for these experiments. You should also have available at least one unadorned wall, or a door which leads into a darkned room. And, yes – privacy. The presence of skeptics dooms one to failure, expecially in the beginning.

STEP TWO

With that taken care of, the next step is to sit quietly and comfortably, and direct your eyes to some single place in the room. This is necessary so that the cloud may collect at the place where you are staring. If you glance here for a moment, and there for a moment, the cloud will not build up. The effect of directed attention is cumulative. The longer you look in the same direction, the more definite the cloud you are building becomes.

STEP THREE

Now since the cloud is, after all, a subtle phenomenon – else it would not make you invisible – we are going to have to apply the principles we studied in earlier chapters for enhancing sight. That means de-focusing the eyes slightly as we stare and wait for the cloud to become apparent. H. Spencer Lewis, who discusses this technique in his 'Ninth Degree' monographs, suggests that you look beyond anything that might be in front of you, as if you were looking at something five miles away. He calls this 'passive visual perception', and he refers to the point also made by both Butler and Bates – that the eyes see better when they are passive. By slightly de-focusing your eyes, you will enhance your ability to see the cloud. And for the same reason that near-sighted people throw away their glasses and others learn to see the aura.

Lewis suggests that you keep your eyes half open while you stare and wait for the cloud to collect, but I find that one additional principle is necessary for me to get results. My eyes tend to focus on whatever is in front of me, despite my efforts to prevent it, and to keep that from happening, I sit in front of something that simply is not worth looking at.

I have had good results looking at a plain white wall, whereas others prefer a dark background. Schrenk-Notzing noted that for some, the cloud shows up better against something dark, and you may wish to use a dark cloth or a doorway into an unlit room. Practically anything will work just so long as it is so *nil* to your eyes that they tend to de-focus naturally after a few moments of concentration. Collecting the cloud is of no use to you if you cannot see it after it is collected. Therefore, this de-focusing is absolutely essential to the technique.

STEP FOUR

If you have absolute privacy, and I do mean *absolute* privacy, you might want to do some chanting along with the staring and the de-focusing. I personally find this unnecessary and even distracting, but H. Spencer Lewis recommended it to his disciples, and you might want to try it if you have difficulty getting results without it.

The *mantra* to use here is RA-MA. It is the name of a Hindu god, and it is the name of an Egyptian god, and it is also the name of the city where the School of the Prophets was founded in ancient Palestine. H. Spencer Lewis says that the syllable RA represents the positive, masculine energy in the universe, and that MA represents the negative, feminine potency. Together, they represent the creative power that brought the universe into existence out of the *cloud* in the beginning. By chanting these syllables together, we bring some of that creative power into the present day, and once again call into existence that cloud out of which the Cosmos was formed.

Each syllable should be drawn out, thus: RAHHHHHHHHH-MAHHHHHHHHH and should be repeated fifteen or twenty times per session. As you chant the *mantra*, bear in mind that you are trying to bring together the dual sex potencies in the universe and produce a manifestation thereby.[22]

STEP FIVE

At this point I may as well be honest with you and tell you that all of this will not fall into place the very first time you do it. I have had people tell me that they tried fifty times or more before they started getting results. Anything worth doing is worth doing repeatedly. But the cloud can be formed, and has been formed hundreds of times by the Wise.

Now the biggest problem that you will have is not producing the cloud, but recognizing that you *are* producing the cloud. Sometimes you will be concentrating and you will see what appear to be heat waves, radiating from the spot where you are staring. If you see this, congratulations! That is not it!

It is what H. Spencer Lewis described as a faint discolouration of the atmosphere, nothing more. If you are using a white background, the cloud will appear to be a very, very faint blue stain that almost cannot be seen at all. The one thing that will tell you for certain when you are getting results is that anything on the other side of the cloud will be blotted out.

The first time I got results with this experiment, I was lying in bed recovering from influenza, and using the ceiling of my bedroom for a backdrop. I was wondering silently how much longer I should have to work to get success with this phenomenon, when I suddenly noticed that a very slight indentation in the ceiling where I was staring could no longer be seen. This indentation was quite visible before – you tend to notice such things after staring at them for some time – and when I looked more closely, I noticed that there was a very subtle blue haze between the ceiling and my eyes. If I looked away from the target area, I could see the ceiling quite clearly. If I looked where this blue haze was forming, I could see nothing. However, if I had looked for the cloud itself, I would never have noticed it. It was almost invisible.

When you think you are getting results, it is time for step five — building the cloud. There are several different ways in which this may be accomplished. You will recall that the Buddhist nun mentioned by Madame Blavatsky in chapter two 'began to draw together, by large handfuls as it were, invisible material from the surrounding atmosphere'. Some people do have excellent results using their hands in this experiment, and there is a technique that is widely used in Western secret orders based on this principle.

The idea is to start with your hands separated by a foot and a half or so, then bring them together, at the same time holding in mind the thought that you are compressing the astral material in the space between them. You are not to gather anything, precisely. The motion that you will make is rather like that of a man playing an accordion. You bring your hands together, then drawn them apart, then bring them together again.

This technique was once used by members of the Inner Peace Movement, and a woman connected with that movement told me that she could see balls of light forming in the space between her hands when she did this experiment. Some people get excellent results using this method. As for myself, I get nothing whatever.

A method which works better for me is based on will power and eye movement, and does not involve the hands in any way at all. After you have once seen the cloud begin to form, look away from it, allow the energy to collect in another region of space, and after a moment or two, bring your eyes gradually toward the centre, where the main cloud is forming, at the same time *willing* that the energy in other parts of the room will move in and join with the energy already in the cloud. You may glance up above the cloud, then bring your eyes down, willing that the energy above the cloud be added to the energy of the cloud itself, then do the same thing by glancing below the cloud, then to either side of it. Remember as you do this that your willing is not to involve eye strain in any way. The willing must be entirely mental. The eyes must remain passive if you are to see what you are doing.

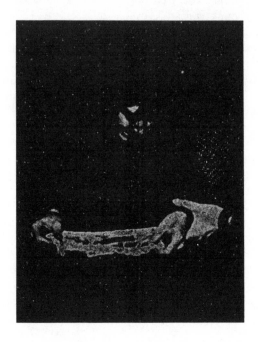

Eva C. using her hands to build up the *cloud*. From Shrenk-Notzing, *Materializationsphänomene* (1914).

You may find it helpful to mix this technique with step number two, and start the building-up process at the same time you start the concentration that allows the cloud to collect in the first place. In other words, rather than concentrate until you can see something visible beginning to collect you might want to alternate between steps one and five, concentrating for a few moments, then building up the cloud for a few moments, and then returning to your concentration. This helps relieve the tedium that often accompanies occult experiments, and can produce some excellent results.

STEP SIX

After you have produced the cloud successfully, you will discover that it has a natural tendency to disperse to the four corners of your room. This is according to the laws of thermodynamics, and if you allow it to happen, eventually the energy in the cloud will become evenly distributed throughout the surrounding space. This dispersing action takes the form of a *spin*, and must be countered by another spin of opposite type if the cloud is to be of any use to you.

The dispersing spin takes place in a *clockwise direction*, and you must counter it by willing that the cloud spin in a *anti-clockwise* direction. Once it starts to do this, rather than becoming larger and thinner, it will become smaller and more dense. Therefore, you may need to alternate this step with step five, causing a anti-clockwise spin, then building up more energy into the cloud as it shrinks.

If you persist with this, you may build a cloud that is very dense indeed. This is one of the secrets of materialization, and I have been told of an AMORC Grand Master who has completely blotted out the light of a 150 watt bulb in private demonstrations using this method. The Frenchman A. Secour has compared this process with the formation of *nebulae* in outer space. Astronomers contend that galaxies, including our own, are formed in this way, with gigantic clouds spinning and condensing until they gradually form suns and planets.[23]

STEP SEVEN

Once you have formed a cloud that is quite definite and which contains a great deal of astral substance, the final step is to draw it around yourself and blot yourself out of view. Once again, the technique is just the logical result of everything we have said thus far. You must produce a cloud large enough to enshroud the human body, then *will* that it come toward you and surround you. If there is a tendency for it to shine, you may want to *will* that it assume a neutral colour, perhaps the same colour as your surroundings. I have never noticed this effect myself, but it has been mentioned by numerous others, especially ancient authors. In *The Six Keys*, Euxodus says of it that 'it is properly called the *great Lunaria*, because of the brightness with which it shines'. If you get this result, you will want to suppress it with your will power. It is no use trying to become invisible in a lighthouse.

When you think that you can make yourself invisible, it is well to have a small mirror in your laboratory, placed perhaps six or seven feet away so that you can see your own image in it. If after you form the cloud and surround yourself with it, you can no longer see yourself in the mirror, you are getting objective results. I must caution you about inviting friends to come into your laboratory to see if they can see you. After you have achieved perfect mastery of the experiment, this kind of thing is fine. But at first, when you are still getting results sporadically, you may repeat the experience of Lord Lytton and make yourself ridiculous instead.

As you advance, you might want to try some elementary experiments in materialization, perhaps producing lights in your room or columns of smoke, or even images. As Vaughan said, 'it is to no purpose to know this Matter unless we know the thing itself to which the notion relates. We must see it, handle it, and by experimental ocular demonstration know the very central invisible essences and properties of it.'[24] This can come only from experience.

Now there is one other effect that can be produced with the cloud that does not lend itself to experimentation, but I want to make mention of it nonetheless. This is invulnerability. In times of danger, you may surround yourself with the cloud, and thereby protect yourself, not only by making yourself invisible, but by physically isolating yourself from whatever the danger is. As Madame Blavatsky interprets this phenomenon:

The astral fluid can be compressed about a person so as to form an elastic shell, absolutely non-penetrable by any physical object, however great the velocity with which it travels. In a word, this fluid can be made to equal and even excel in resisting power, water and air.

In India, Malabar, and some places of Central Africa, the conjurers will freely permit any traveller to fire his musket or revolver at them, without touching the weapon themselves or selecting the balls. In Laing's *Travels Among the Timanni, the Kourankos, and the Soulimas,* occurs a description by an English traveller, the first white man to visit the tribe of the Soulimas, of a very curious scene. A body of picked soldiers fired upon a chief who had nothing to defend himself with but certain talismans. Although their muskets were properly loaded and aimed, not a ball could strike him. Salverte gives a similar case in his *Philosophy of Occult Sciences:* 'In 1568 the Prince of Orange condemned a Spanish prisoner to be shot at Juliers; the soldiers tied him to a tree and fired, but he was invulnerable. They at last stripped him to see what armour he wore, but found only an *amulet.* When this was taken from him, *he fell dead at the first shot.*'

This is a very different affair from the dexterous trickery resorted to by Houdin in Algeria. He prepared balls himself of tallow, blackened with soot, and by sleight of hand exchanged them for real bullets, which the Arab sheikhs supposed they were putting in the pistols. The simple-minded natives, knowing nothing but real magic, which they had inherited from their ancestors, and seeing Houdin, as they thought, accomplish the same results in a more impressive manner, fancied that he was a greater magician than themselves. Many travellers, the writer included, have witnessed instances of this invulnerability where deception was impossible. A few years ago, there lived in an African village an Abyssinian, who passed for a sorcerer. Upon one occasion a party of Europeans, going to Sudan, amused themselves for an hour or two in firing at him with their own pistols and muskets, a privilege which he gave them for a trifling fee. As many as five shots were fired simultaneously, and the muzzles of the pieces were not above two yards distant from the sorcerer's breast. In each case, simultaneously with the flash, the bullet would appear just behind the muzzle, quivering in the air, and then fall harmlessly to the ground. A German offered the magician a five franc piece if he would allow him to fire the gun with the muzzle touching his body. The magician at first refused, but finally, after appearing to hold conversation with someone inside the ground, consented. The experimenter carefully loaded, and, pressing the muzzle of the weapon against the sorcerer's body, fired. The barrel burst into fragments as far down as the stock, and the magician walked off unhurt.

In our own time several well-known mediums have frequently, in the presence of the most respectable witnesses, not only handled blazing coals and actually placed their faces upon a fire without singing a hair, but even laid flaming coals upon the heads and hands of bystanders, as in the case of Lord Lindsay and Lord Adare. The well-known story of the Indian chief, who confessed to Washington that at Braddock 's defeat he fired his rifle at him seventeen times without effect, will recur to the reader in this connection.[25]

This effect has been demonstrated in Europe as well, but as I said, it is not something that one would want to deliberately make use of as an experiment. It is something to keep in mind; one more effect produced by the marvellous power of the *cloud*.

8. Disappearing à la Patanjali

H. Spencer Lewis was not one for telling his sources, but from some references in the Rosicrucian monographs, one could infer that the technique for forming the cloud is an *Oriental* one, at least in origin. We are told that invisibility demonstrations take place 'in some lands, such as India', and we are told in another place that the cloud is specifically the method by which the *Hindus* make themselves invisible. Lewis was in contact with several persons who studied occult sciences in India during his lifetime, and we shall find that if we pursue this Oriental connection, we shall make some interesting discoveries indeed.

One of these is that invisibility is not usually connected with the Orient. India is, of course, one of the two traditional homes of occultism, the other being Egypt; but whereas *levitation* is usually thought of as an Oriental achievement, *invisibility* is actually more Western in flavour. Medieval witches commonly made themselves invisible, or so say their persecutors; fakirs and saddhus do not.

One is tempted to suspect that Lewis' thinking may have been affected by a popular radio programme that was aired extensively in the USA during the 1930s. The hero of the programme was Lamont Cranston, who learned secrets in the Orient whereby he could walk invisibly among men, and who returned to the West as 'the Shadow', learning what evil might lurk in the hearts of men. This programme was an important part of popular culture, and may well have influenced otherwise well-informed people to believe that ordinary Indians walk invisibly, just as Lamont Cranston did. But even if invisibility is not so specifically an Indian phenomenon as levitation is, the Indians were no stranger to it, and there are some interesting stories of invisibility in India that may lend some support to Lewis' assertion.

The most interesting of these centre around Apollonius of Tyana, a first-century Greek sage who visited India in the company of his disciple, Damis. Quoting from Damis' diaries, Philostratus tells us that the pair discovered a Brahman monastery which was situated on a hill of about the same size and elevation as that which supported the Acropolis in Athens. He also says that 'they saw a *cloud* floating round the eminence on which the Indians live', and that by its means '*they render themselves visible or invisible*'. They were unable to determine 'whether there were any other gates to the eminence ... for the *cloud* around it did not allow [the gates] anywhere to be seen, whether there was an opening in the rampart, or whether on the other hand it was a close-shut fortress.'[1] Thomas Vaughan compares this with the House *Sanctus Spiritus* of the Rosicrucians.[2] It was obviously a suitable place for the meeting of high Adepts, and it appears from Philostratus that Apollonius was taught the secret of the *cloud's* formation, because on his return to the West he demonstrated the power himself.

The Emperor Domitian had Apollonius arrested, as tyrants are wont to do, and demanded that he appear before the imperial court to answer a long series of trumped-up charges. An absurd trial followed, at which the magician defended himself, and when it became obvious to even Apollonius that the whole thing was a farce, he quoted a verse from the *Iliad* in which he announced that he was not mortal, and 'vanished from the court'.[3]

The emperor was of course astonished, as well he might have been, but even more astonished were Apollinius' disciples. For one hour after he vanished from Domitian's court, Apollonius appeared to them at the grotto of Puteoli, *a journey of several days distance.*

Speculating on this remarkable feat, Madame Blavatsky surmises in *Isis Unveiled* that: '[Apollonius'] physical body having become invisible by the concentration of *Akasa* about it, he could walk off unperceived to some secure retreat in the neighbourhood, and an hour after his astral form appear at Puteoli to his friends, and seem to be the man himself.'[4]

This is undoubtedly the correct interpretation, and it is particularly interesting because it lends support to the theory that Apollonius vanished by means of the *cloud*. As I pointed out in chapter three, the Hindu *Akasa* is the equivalent of the alchemist's *First Matter*, and is therefore the material of which the *cloud* is composed. Madame Blavatsky's assertion that Apollonius' body became invisible 'by the concentration of *Akasa* about it' could therefore have been lifted straight out of some medieval Rosicrucian manuscript, with the alteration of a single word – *Akasa*. But it was not. In fact, it was lifted out of a medieval *Indian* manuscript – Vyasa's commentary on the *Yoga Sutras* of Patanjali.

In Book Three of the *Yoga Sutras*, Patanjali discusses the various *Siddhis*, or occult powers, that come to the advanced Yogi through the practice of *Sanyama*. In *Sutras* forty-three and forty-four we are told that subjugation of the Five Elements or *Tattwas* comes from using them as an object. The Yogi can plunge into the Earth as if it were mere Water; he may enter a stone if he wishes; the waters do not wet him; fire does not burn him; and, most of all 'the *Akasa*, which by its very nature covers nothing, will cover him so perfectly that even the *Siddhas* may not see him.' This is an obvious reference to the *cloud*, albeit a carefully veiled one, and upon reflection we can see that H. Spencer Lewis' technique for forming the *cloud* may just be an ingenious interpretation of Vyasa's commentary.

Those of you who have read my previous book, on Levitation, will know that *Sanyama* is merely a process of sustained concentration. There is of course a good deal of theory that goes with the technique, but in practice all one needs to know to do *Sanyama* is to choose an object, get started, and stay with it.

Now suppose that we wanted to do an open-eye *Sanyama* on the space surrounding us – the *Akasa*. We would sit quietly, perhaps in one of the classical meditation poses, open our eyes, and look into space, but without concentrating on any specific object. We would want to look, but we would not want to look *at* anything. That way, we could ensure that our *Sanyama* is on space, and not on anything contained in it. And to do that, we would want to look beyond whatever might be in front of us, perhaps de-focusing our eyes slightly. Obviously, this is what we do when we form the *cloud*, and for that reason the process of forming the cloud might be thought of as a *Sanyama* on the *Akasa*.

This is significant because Vyasa adds some interesting points that we have not yet considered. We have already seen that after the *cloud* is formed, we must learn to control it with our minds, and make it move through space, spin around, grow larger or smaller, and change colour, for it to be useful. Now in doing this you might think that your mind is operating on the substance of the *cloud* itself, but Vyasa maintains that that is not so. Instead, your mind works on the subtle basis and reorders the process of its evolution.

The idea here is that each of the Five Elements is the result of a process that takes place on the subtler planes. Only the end result of the process is visible, and there are therefore subtler elements which stand behind the gross elements as it were, and which represent invisible, pre-material stages of development. Unlike the gross elements, the subtler elements are susceptible to mental influence, and if we use that influence to affect the evolution of the gross elements, argues Vyasa, the gross elements will follow 'just as a cow follows her calf'.

There is a similar idea in the Western tradition. In *The Great Art* Dom Pernety argues that: 'The perceptible bodies of Earth, Air, Fire, and Water, which in their spheres are really distinct, are not the first and simple elements which Nature employs in her different generations. They seem to be only the matrix of others. The simple elements are imperceptible, until their union forms a dense matter, which we call body, to which are joined the gross elements as integral parts.'[5]

Madame Blavatsky has the very same idea in her *Isis Unveiled*, where she intimates that she found it in the writings of the Rosicrucians:

Fire, in the ancient philosophy of all times and countries, has been regarded as a triple principle. As Water comprises a visible fluid with invisible gases lurking within, and behind all [of these] the spiritual principle of nature, which gives them their dynamic energy, so in Fire [the alchemists] recognized: 1st. Visible flame; 2nd. Invisible, or astral Fire – invisible when inert, but when active producing heat, light, chemical force, and electricity; 3rd. Spirit. They applied the same rule to each of the elements, and everything evolved from their combinations and correlations, man included, was held by them to be triune.[6]

Now the 'invisible gases lurking within' the Water Element are of course hydrogen and oxygen. But it seems clear that the three principles of the elements Madame Blavatsky refers to are the three principles of the alchemists, and it is in alchemical theory that we will find the clearest exposition of these ideas.

You will recall that the alchemists' three principles were esoterically signified by Salt, Sulphur, and Mercury – body, soul, and spirit. Now in *The Book of Alze* these three are shown arranged in the shape of an equilateral triangle, with the Latin names of each of the three principles – Spiritus, Anima, and Corpus – at the triangle's three points, and within a circle containing the names of the seven stages of the Work, and the symbols of the seven metals. In his *Histoire de la Magie* Eliphas Lévi calls this 'the Great Hermetic Arcanum' and attributes it to Basil Valentine. A similar diagram may be found in places in *The Secret Symbols of the Rosicrucians*.

If we redraw this diagram and eliminate all the superfluous symbolism, we have something likes this:

SULPHUR . . . . .MERCURY

SALT

This suggests that the two principles represented by Sulphur and Mercury exist together on a plane above the material, and that they descend together toward the material plane to produce a material

De

LAPIDE PHILOSO-
PHICO

PERBREVE OPUS.
CULUM,

QUOD AB IGNOTO ALIQUO GER-
manico Philofopho, pene ante ducentos annos,
conſcripum & LIBER ALZE nuncupatum fuit,
nunc vero in lucem editum.

FRANCOFURTI
Apud HERMANNUM à SANDE.

Anno MDC LXXVII.

The Law of the Triangle. From *The Book of Alze* in the *Musaeum Hermeticum*.

manifestation, represented esoterically by Salt. Sulphur and Mercury may therefore be thought of as two polarities of subtle manifestation, Sulphur being the masculine principle, and Mercury being feminine. And as such they constitute Vyasa's suble counterparts of the visible elements.

Other sources suggest a more hierarchical arrangement. They speak of Mercury as an intermediate principle, which stands between Sulphur on the higher plane, and Salt on the lower. This is the meaning of the figure in the *Musaeum Hermeticum* in which Mercury is represented by the Greek god with that name, and Sulphur and Salt are shown to either side of him, represented by the Sun and the Moon. Mercury stands between the Sun and the Moon – Sulphur and Salt – and therefore 'mediates' between them.

If we retain the planes concept, though, we shall have to show the three principles stacked one atop the other, thus:

SULPHUR

MERCURY

SALT

This suggests that Sulphur, Mercury, and Salt represent three different planes of manifestation, instead of the two suggested by the triangle, and that Sulphur must first descend toward the 'intermediate' plane designated by Mercury before they can descend together to the material plane represented by Salt.

Now that suggests, further, that Sulphur is what Franz Hartmann called 'the principle of corporification' – that principle which is responsible for starting the process of condensation in Mercury – the *cloud* – which eventually results in a material manifestation. This is why Bonus of Ferrara calls Sulphur 'the proper coagulum of quicksilver'.[7] Quicksilver is, of course, another name for Mercury, which is another name for the *cloud*, and coagulation is another name for condensation. Says Euxodus in *The Six Keys:* 'To corporify the Spirit, which is our Mercury, you must have well dissolved the body in which *the Sulphur which coagulates the Mercury* is enclosed.'[8]

Another word for condensation is 'fixation', as in 'volatilize that

Mercurius between the Opposites. From the *Musaeum Hermeticum*.

which is fixed, and fix that which is volatile.' That which is solid in alchemy is said to be 'fixed'. Of the two subtle principles, the alchemists were fond of saying that Sulphur was 'fixed' and Mercury was 'volatile', 'which, acting upon one another, are volatilized and fixed reciprocally into a perfect Fixity'.[9]

Left to itself, the First Matter would be perpetually unformed and unmanifest, invisible. It is only when it is ensouled, or, as the scholastics would say, 'informed', which is to say, invested with a form, that the process of condensation takes place. In its primordial state, the First Matter is esoterically called 'the sea of the Wise, passive to all impressions and influences of the Light'.[10] And that gives us a clue as to just what the form, the principle esoterically represented by Sulphur and soul, really is: it is mind.

After considering the ectoplasmic phenomena of the séance room, Conan Doyle wrote in his *History of Spiritualism* that 'all the new evidence points to matter being the result of thought'.[11] But that poses a most uncomfortable question that Conan Doyle himself raised in the very next sentence: *Whose thought?*

The religionist will of course say God, and I do not wish to challenge that here. But I would like to offer a somewhat more sophisticated answer, which was accepted by the alchemists, and which is accepted as well by the fakirs and Yogis of the Far East.

It is characteristic of modern man's alienation from Nature that he tends to think of himself as somehow supernatural, in the sense of being *in* Nature, but not *part* of it. Therefore, when he thinks of mind, he thinks of it as something within himself, shared only by other men. He does not think of mind as something that one would find in a rock or a tree.

However, when the alchemist thinks of mind, he thinks of it as something which all of us share, but that none of us owns. It is a universal principle in nature. In a way the mind of man is like the body of man. Each of us possesses a body, and yet the stuff of which it is made – the dust of the earth – is universal. Likewise, each of us possesses a mind, and yet the mind-stuff of which it is made – like the dust of the earth – is universal, diffused throughout nature. When we experience the material world through sensation, we are experiencing a reality that is universal, and so it is with mind. Experience of thought is experience of a universal process.

In fact, it is even more than that. It is experience of a *pre-material* reality. Because mind, whatever it is, preceded the manifestation of the visible universe.

Our error is in tending to identify with mind. I tend to think of my mind as being me, yet the word 'me' refers to the Self, which transcends mind, and which merely observes the acitivity of mind, just as it observes the activity of matter through sensation. The Self may be able to direct mind's powers, and then again it may not. But the first step toward Enlightenment is recognizing the distinction between the two.

Now since mind is not matter, the alchemists posited the existence of what Jung calls 'an intermediate realm between mind and matter, i.e., a psychic realm of subtle bodies, whose characteristic it is to manifest themselves in a mental as well as a material form'[12] As Read explained it:

> Gross or tangible matter took shape in progressively finer forms, ranging through mists, smokes, exhalations, air, and the so-called ether, to animal spirits, the soul, and spiritual beings. There was supposed to be an essential unity of all things, whether tangible or intangible, material or spiritual.[13]

The intermediate condition between mind and matter corresponds to the Astral Plane of the occultists. It is the 'spirit' of the alchemists, which mediates between soul — mind — and the body — the material plane, and in its lower aspect it is said to be a perfect copy of the visible universe.

This is the basis for the palingenesis experiment, in which a plant is cremated and then resurrected from its own ashes. It is obvious that for the First Matter to condense into a certain form, that form must exist at the start of the condensation process, in a subtle form, in the Astral Light. After the plant is cremated, the form remains in the Astral Light according to Hartmann 'until those remnants have been fully deomposed, and by certain methods known to the alchemist it may be re-clothed with matter and become visible again'.[14]

As long as the plant is alive, its astral form co-exists with its visible form, and sustains the visible form throughout the plant's life. If the plant is damaged, the astral form remains intact, and by recent development in photography may be made visible, just as the alchemists made these forms visible centuries ago.

The techniques are of course those which were revived by Kirlian in the Soviet Union a few years ago. I say revived because there is an electrophotograph which resembles a Kirlian photograph in Papus' *Magie et l'Hypnose*, first published in 1897. Papus procured this photograph from M. de Narkiewicz Iodko, and identifies it as 'photography of the Od and the astral body', and the description of the manner in which the photograph was made resembles the techniques used in making modern, Kirlian photographs. So it would appear that Kirlian photography is not such a new thing as many recent writers would suggest.[15]

I have personally seen a Kirlian photograph made of a plant leaf from which a portion was amputated with a pair of scissors, and it clearly shows the intactness of the astral form. Because whereas an ordinary photograph would show the plant as it was – with a portion cut off – the Kirlian photograph showed it *as if it were still whole*. There is no question about this phenomenon, and it even manifests in human beings, who have had a limb amputated.

In this case it is known as the 'phantom limb' effect. Quoting a French correspondent of an English journal, Madame Blavatsky mentions 'a gentleman who had an arm amputated at the shoulder' and who 'is certain that he has a spiritual arm, which he sees and actually feels with his other hand. He can touch anything, and even pull up things with the spiritual arm and hand.'[16] She also claims to have known an Eastern Adept who suffered the same misfortune. 'This eminent scholar and practical kabalist [sic] can at will project his astral arm, and with the hand take up, move, and carry objects, even at a considerable distance from where he may be sitting. We have often seen him thus minister to the wants of a favourite elephant.'[17]

Advanced students of astral projection know that when they project into the presence of an amputee, they see the person as if he were still whole, just as Kirlian photography shows the multilated leaf as if it were still whole. I have seen this myself. And that is the basis of occult teaching about the Astral Plane. The secret schools maintain that the 'phantom limb' effect derives from the existence of an actual subtle limb, and they also maintain that it is the plane on which this subtle limb manifests itself – or the Astral Plane – that one really sees when doing projection.

Now as I have said, these three planes have an objective and a subjective aspect. The world of matter has a subjective aspect in sensation. And the world of forms, or soul, or Sulphur, has its subjective aspect in mind. We would therefore expect the Astral Plane to correspond to a subjective category of experience also, and we find that that would be emotion.

In Jung's Analytical Psychology, though, there are said to be, not three, but four categories of conscious experience; thoughts, feeling, sensations, *and* intuitions. Intuitions include everything that cannot be grouped into one of the other three categories – dream experiences, psychic experiences, and so forth – and that suggests that there might be, not three, but four planes of existence.

That is the position taken in the Qabalah, where we read of the four 'Worlds'. The highest of these is Atziluth – the World of Archetypes – which corresponds subjectively to intuition. The lower worlds, which correspond to thoughts, feelings, and sensations, are Briah, Yetzirah, and Malkuth respectively.[18]

Now it appears from certain obscure references that the Qabalists were familiar with the formation of the *cloud*, because, as Manly Hall says:

> In the Mysteries Adam is accredited with having the peculiar power of spiritual generation. Instead of reproducing his kind by the physical generative processes, he caused to issue from himself – or, more correctly, to be reflected upon substance – a shadow of himself. This shadow he then ensouled and it became a living creature.[19]

In another version of this 'the Elohim gazed down into the Abyss [and] beheld their own shadows, and from these shadows patterned the inferior creation.'[20] This is the origin of the expression 'shadowed forth'. The shadows are obviously less substantial than the creation, just as the *cloud* is less substantial than matter. Yet the subtle precedes the gross in either case.

When we posit the existence of a plane higher than the mental, we are merely recognizing the fact that the mind of man is not man himself any more than the body is. It is merely a part of his lower nature. The true essence of man is represented by the highest of the four Worlds, and transcends all of the lower three.

This idea is most lucidly developed in the *Samkhya* system of Hindu philosophy, and with that we have just come full circle – from the notions of the alchemists all the way back to Vyasa and Patanjali. The terminology is somewhat different, but the underlying concepts are quite consistent from one system to the other. And it is important for us to understand *Samkhya* concepts, because they form the theoretical basis of Yoga itself.

The *Samkhya* philosophy is one of the six orthodox systems of Hindu philosophy. It was founded by an ancient sage named Kapila, about whom we know nothing, and none of whose writings have survived. *Samkhya* authorities say that the original *Samkhya-Sutras* have long since vanished from the earth, but we do have a few texts which are very old, such as the *Tattva-samasa*, which are believed to reflect Kapila's original teaching.

Kapila was essentially concerned with the problem of matter, just as were the alchemists, the Qabalists, and the Rosicrucians, and, like those, he believed that the universe originated through a process of involution, in which subtler principles descended to more gross levels of manifestation, which they both form and support.

In the beginning, he said, there were only two principles: the *Purusha* and the *Prakriti* – the observer and that which is observed. *Purusha* is the soul, and unlike the *Vedanta* philosophers, Kapila assumed that each of us possesses our own soul, separate and distinct from the souls of others. *Prakriti* is usually translated as 'primordial matter'. It is the First Matter of the alchemists, untouched by soul, and as such said to be *A-vyakta* – Unmanifest: 'It has neither beginning, middle, nor end, nor has it any parts. It is inaudible, intangible, invisible, indestructible, eternal, without savour or odour. [It is] subtle, without attributes, producing but unproduced, without parts, one only, but common to all.'[21]

With a few stylistic changes, this statement might have come straight from Raymund Lully or Paracelsus, or even the first of the alchemists – Hermes. In the unmanifest state the three qualities, or *Gunas*, of *Prakriti* are said to be in perfect equilibrium. Now these three *Gunas* are qualities, and they possess the ability to become all the qualities that the First Matter may eventually assume. However, the fact of their being in equilibrium means that the First Matter possesses no qualities at all, or at least that the qualities, which are there potentially, are not yet manifested.

Now this is the same concept as that of the alchemists, but it is expressed more ingeniously, and is more difficult to understand. The alchemist, like the *Samkhya* philosopher, believes that the First Matter has the potential to take on every kind of form. It may become hot and dry, or cold and moist; it may become yellow, green, lavender or beige. But until the form, or the Philosopher's Sulphur, is imposed upon it, it has no qualities whatsoever. It receives all its qualities from the form, which as we have seen, originates with mind.

The *Samkhya* philosophers, on the other hand, say that all the qualities are already in the First Matter, and that all that is required is to bring them out. It is like white light. All the colours of the rainbow are contained in it, but unless we split it apart with a prism, we cannot see them. Likewise, with the First Matter – the *A-vyakta Prakriti* – all the qualities are present, but until one or the other predominates, none of the qualities are manifest. The matter is formless, waiting for shape.

The *Samkhya* also agreed with Western alchemy in assuming that mind was somehow responsible for the shaping, but here again we run into some subtle points. It is obvious that the qualities of the First Matter cannot be manifest unless they are manifest *to* someone. Thus two requirements, and not one, are necessary for manifestation: there must be a disturbance in the equilibrium of the *Gunas*, and there must be someone to whom this disturbance will be apparent.

As Max Müller puts it, not only is there no hearing without sound; there is no sound without hearing. Two things: a disturbance in the world of matter, and a conscious entity, are required to produce sound. And so it goes with other kinds of manifestations.[22]

Now Kapila was unable to decide whether the awareness preceded the disturbance in the *Gunas*, or whether the disturbance in the *Gunas* preceded the awareness, so he merely combined the two. He assumed that the Gunas are in equilibrium until there is awareness. As soon as *Purusha*, who has formerly been in darkness, gazes upon *Prakriti*, the *Gunas* are disturbed. The process of manifestation has begun.

'Some such impulse is required by all metaphysicians,' says Müller. 'This first step in the development of *Prakriti*, this first awakening of the inert substance, is conceived by Kapila as *Buddhi*, the lighting up, and hence, so long as it is confined to *Prakriti*, described as *Prakasa*, or light, the chief condition of all perception.'[23]

The word *Buddhi*, which is not to be confused with *Buddha*, comes from the Sanskrit root *Budh*, which means to awaken or to perceive.[24] And the idea that Kapila intends to give here is literally that of awakening to perception. *Purusha*, or the soul, possesses the potential for perception, but cannot actualize that potential unless he has something to perceive. This is what Husserl calls the 'intentionality' of consciousness. Consciousness is always consciousness *of* something. And the *Purusha* can only be conscious of *Prakriti*; else he is not conscious.

Now when *Purusha* gazes upon *Prakriti*, his potential for consciousness is actualized, and *Prakriti* advances from the Unmanifest to the Manifest state, from *A-vyakta* to *Vyakta*. But as we have already said, for him to become Manifest, a disturbance in the three *Gunas* is necessary. Therefore we say that these two take place simultaneously. There is the gazing of *Purusha* upon *Prakriti*, and there is the disturbance of the *Gunas*. Both of these are necessary for manifestation.

Now this manifestation, which takes place when *Purusha* becomes conscious of *Prakriti*, means that a third thing has been brought into existence, which is consciousness itself. This is what the *Samkhya* philosophers call *Buddhi*.

'*Buddhi* [is] commonly translated by perception,' writes Müller, 'but is really a kind of perception that involves something like what we should call intellect (*nous*).'[25] Intellect is of course one of the potentialities of *Purusha*, as is consciousness, and arises at the same time and for the same reason. '*Buddhi* exists in human nature as the power of perception,' Müller continues, 'and it is then, though not quite correctly, identified with *Manas*, the mental activity going on within us, which combines and regulates the impressions of the senses. But as a cosmic force, *Buddhi* is that which gives light as the essential condition of all knowledge, and is afterwards developed into the senses, the powers of light and thought.'[26] After *Prakriti* has been thus lighted up and become *Buddhi*, or potential perception, 'another distinction was necessary in this luminous and perceiving mass, namely, the differentiation between perceiver and what is perceived, between subject and object.'[27] This is technically known as *Ahamkara*, which means 'the production of Ego', or 'the production of a sense of the "I" '. It is the beginning of Self-awareness, and it implies the beginning of other-awareness, because as Max Müller explains: 'Though *Ahamkara* means only the production of Ego, yet the production of Ego involves that of the Non-Ego, and thus divides the whole world into what is subjective and objective.'[28]

If I have a sense of the 'I', which is to say, if my awareness includes an awareness of myself as a separate person, that necessarily implies an awareness of the distinction between myself, the 'I', and things which are not me. This is necessary according to Müller because:

> *Buddhi* cannot really act without a distinction of the universe into subject and object, without the introduction of the Ego or I, which again is impossible without a Non-Ego, or something objective. After that only do we watch the development of what is objective in general into what is objectively this or that (*Tanmatras*).[29]

At this point, the fact that there are three *Gunas* becomes important for the first time, because *Ahamkara* develops into one of three forms, depending on which of the three *Gunas* is in the ascendancy. These are the *Vaikarika*, 'modifying', *Taigasa*, 'luminous', and *Bhutadi*, 'the first of elements'.[30] They correspond respectively to the *Sattva, Rajas,* and *Tamas Gunas* and produce *Tanmatras*, the *Indriyas*, and the *Mahabhutas*, again respectively.[31]

At this point I think it might be worthwhile to diagram the

development of matter according to the *Samkhya* philosophy.

PURUSHA . . . . AVYAKTA
                          .   .   PRAKRITI

            .   .

            .   .
                .

BUDDHI

(Intellect and Perception)

|

AHAMKARA

(Consciousness of the 'I')

Takes on three aspects according to the Gunas:

Vaikarika Modifying (Sattva Guna)	Bhutadi First of Elements (Tamas Guna)	Taigasa Luminous (Rajas Guna)
	Produces:	
The five Tanmatras	The five Mahabhutas	Mahat and the Indriyas

As you can see, *Purusha* and *A-vyakta Prakriti*, Soul and the First Matter, come together to produce *Buddhi* at the third and lowest point of the triangle. *Buddhi* then becomes *Ahamkara*, which, according to which *Guna* is dominant, produces either the *Tanmatras*, the *Indriyas* plus *Manas*, or the *Mahabhutas*.

Now as you remember, *Ahamkara* is actually a division into two, the 'I' and the 'Not-I', or, if you will, the perceiver and the perceived. And we shall find that this division into three aspects is actually a division into subjective and objective, with the objective being two-fold.

Thus, the five *Mahabhutas* are the five gross elements, the five *Tattwas-Akasa, Vayu, Tejas, Apas,* and *Prithivi.* They manifest themselves when the *Tamas Guna,* which represents inertia, becomes dominant in the trio. The five *Mahabhutas* are products, or condensations, if you will, of the five *Tanmatras,* which are the five subtle elements, or *Sukshma-Bhutas.* These are the five subtle elements which were mentioned by Vyasa in his commentary on the *Yoga Sutras,* and which were also mentioned by Dom Pernety in *The Great Art.*

The *Tanmatras* are in effect the astral counterparts of the five gross elements. According to Theos Bernard, the word *Tanmatra* comes from the Sanskrit *tad,* meaning 'that', and *matra,* which means *'element'.*[32] 'These subtle elements are the subtle forms of matter.' writes Dr. Bernard, 'and are referred to as mere dream stuff.'[33] They are 'the subtlest objects of the sense powers, the subtlest forms of actual matter, without magnitude, supersensible, and perceived mediately only through gross objects.'[34]

The Maharishi Mahesh Yogi says in his commentary on the *Bhagavad-Gita* that 'the *tanmatras* mark a dividing line between the subjective and objective creation ... the *tanmatras,* forming as they do, the basis of the five elements, lie in the grossest field of the subjective aspect of creation.'[35] It is said in the texts that you see them when you press your fingertips against the lids of your closed eyes.[36]

Now this is one of the places at which occult science and orthodox science diverge. Orthodox, materialistic, scientists explain the light that one sees when pressing against the eyelids by saying that the pressure causes the cells in the retina to fire randomly, producing light sensations without actual light stimulation. But whoever is right – and I do not wish personally to take a stand here – it is a fact that this form of colour perception is somehow connected with psychic sight. Says Babbitt:

Those who are developed to see the odic and higher lights see these colours with incomparably greater vividness and diversity than those who are not. This is especially true in my own experience. Before being able to see these high grade colours, I rarely ever saw any glimpse of colour with my eyes closed, even under pressure, but since the development of this vision I can see them vividly, on the merest touch, and still more vividly by closing my eyes and looking in a single direction for some time. Some persons are not conscious of ever having seen these colours.[37]

The *Tanmatras* are also connected in some way with ordinary sight, as well as the other ordinary senses. Since in the *Samkhya* system the formation of matter is a process of involution of mind into matter, it follows that consciousness should arise at the same time as matter. The two go together. In fact, in Müller's interpretation, the *Tanmatras* are just a further refinement of the idea expressed by *Ahamkara*. After the distinction of 'this and that' in general – represented by the *Ahamkara* – there is the distinction of 'this and that' in particular, represented by the *Tanmatras*.[38] As the *Tamas Guna* becomes stronger in its influence, the five *Tanmatras* condense and solidify into the five elements – the five *Mahabhutas* – which are called 'gross' elements, the word 'gross' meaning 'perceptible to the senses'.[39] Each of these 'gross' elements is connected with a particular *Tanmatra*, which is in turn connected with a particular sense, thus:

Sattva Guna	Tamas Guna	Rajas Guna	
Tanmatra	Mahabhuta	Jnanendriya	Karmendriya
Sabda	Akasa (Space)	Srota (Hearing)	Vak (Speaking)
Sparsa	Vayu (Air)	Tvak (Touch)	Pani (Grasping)
Rupa	Tejas (Fire)	Caksus (Sight)	Pada (Walking)
Rasa	Apas (Water)	Gihva (Taste)	Payu (Eliminating)
Gandha	Prithivi (Earth)	Ghrana (Smell)	Upastha (Sex)

Senses are considered in *Samkhya* to be of two sorts: active and passive. Thus under the *Rajas Guna* we find the passive, receptive sense of hearing coupled with the active sense of speaking. The Maharishi Mahesh Yogi explains that the *Tanmatras* are considered to be the 'essences' of the senses, and in *Nature's Finer Forces*, Rama Prasad tells us that the *Mahabhutas*, which are also called *Tattwas*, are the 'ethers'.[40] Thus *Tejas* is the 'luminiferous ether' of nineteenth-century science, and the others are 'ethers' science knows nothing about. *Akasa* is the 'sonoriferous' ether, *Apas* is the 'gustiferous' ether, and so on.[41]

Now all of this is the basis of practical yogic occultism. As the Maharishi Mahesh Yogi pointed out: 'The whole teaching of Kapila's *Samkhya* can be verified by direct experience through Transcendental Meditation, because in order to reach the state of transcendental consciousness the mind has to traverse all the gross and subtle states of creation.'[42] By doing this deliberately, the yogi acquires mastery over the Elements, including the *Akasa*, and can thereby make himself invisible. The actual technique is hinted at by Patanjali in the forty-third *Sutra* of the *Yoga Sutras:* 'Mastery of the Elements is acquired by Sanyama on the gross (*sthula*), the substantive (*svarupa*), the astral (*sukshma*), the conjunction (*anvaya*), and the purposefulness (*arthavattva*).'[43] You will notice that there are five of these states of matter. They correspond *almost*, but not quite, to the five stages outlined by Kapila.

The 'gross' is what Kapila would have called the *Mahabhuta*, that in the Elements which is perceptible to the senses. The 'substantive' is what Ganganatha Jha described as 'their respective generic characteristic: shape for the Earth, viscidity for the Water, heat for Fire, velocity for Air, and omnipresence for the *Akasa*.'[44] The generic characteristics are visible in a way, but unlike the gross, they are not substantial. Hence, they are considered separately in yoga.

Vyasa makes it clear in his commentary that the 'astral' forms are the *Tanmatras*. The 'conjunction' is the conjunction of the three *Gunas*, and the 'purposefulness' has to do with the *Purusha*.

'The Yogi makes Sanyama ... first on the gross, and then on the finer states,' wrote Vivekananda.

> They take a lump of clay and make *Sanyama* on that, and gradually they begin to see the fine materials of which it is composed. When they have known all the fine materials in it, they get power over that element. So with all the elements. The Yogi can conquer them all.[45]

Depending on how far you get with this process, you are promised one or more of the Eight Great Siddhis – according to tradition.

The first four come from *Sanyama* on the gross, perceptible form, thus

(1) *Anima* – the power to become as small as the atom;
(2) *Laghima* – extreme lightness, levitation;
(3) *Mahima* – the power to become infinitely large;
(4) *Prapti* – the power to touch the Moon with your fingertips.

The remaining four come from *Sanyama* on the subtler forms of the Elements:

(5) *Prakamya* – wish-fulfillment by mere thought, comes from *Sanyama* on the generic characteristic. The Yogi with *Prakamya* may dive into the Earth as if it were Water.
(6) *Vasitva* – Mastery of the Elements and their products, without being mastered in turn. Comes from *Sanyama* on the *Tanmatras*.
(7) *Isitva* – control over the appearance, the disappearance, and the arrangement of the Elements. Comes from *Sanyama* on the *Gunas*.
(8) *Yatrakamavasayitva* – Lordship. Comes from *Sanyama* on the *Purusha*.

According to the *Siva Samhita*, invisibility comes from acquisition of *Prakamya*, and of course *Prakamya* comes from *Sanyama* on the *Tanmatras*.[46]

This just gets us back to what Vyasa said about controlling the Elements through their subtle bases. If we are going to form the cloud, we must achieve some mental control over the substance of the cloud, and we have seen that that substance is the *Akasa Tattwa*. Vyasa assumes that when we assert mental control over any Element, we are really acting upon the *subtle basis* of that Element. The subtle basis of any Element is the corresponding *Tanmatra*, and the subtle basis of the Akasa is the *Sabda Tanmatra*. Thus we would only expect that *Prakamya* would lead directly to invisibility.

There is another way in which this information may be applied, however, and that is suggested in one of Patanjali's later *Sutras*.

Patanjali says that we can also consider doing *Sanyama* on the senses themselves. Therefore, instead of doing *Sanyama* on the five Elements in their five forms, we do *Sanyama* on the five senses in *their* five forms. We therefore acquire direct power over the sense itself.[47] Invisibility, say, would come from subjugating the sense of sight.

The *Samkhyas* believe that the five senses evolved simultaneously with their five objects. Thus they, like their five objects, are fivefold. And, by the same token, they share the same natures.[48]

The sense of sight, for example, is of the same nature as the *Tejas Tattwa* – Fire. Even the name of the eye in Sanskrit – *caksus* – comes from the roots *caks*, 'to see', and *kas*, 'to shine'.[49] Thus the light from the eyes, which we learned about in the last chapter, was recognized in Eastern as well as Western, thought.

Applying the five categories, and I am following the commentaries here, the 'gross' aspect of sight is simply vision itself. It is the perceptible aspect, and the perceptible aspect of perception is just that – perception.

The 'generic' aspect is visibility, the quality of being visible. The subtle basis is the *Rupa Tanmatra*, which signifies both colour and form. The 'conjunction' is the *Sattva Guna*, one quality of which is luminosity. And the 'purposiveness' of sight has to do with the *Purusha* as being capable potentially of awareness.

Just as it is not necessary to acquire all of the Eight *Siddhis* to produce the cloud, though, so too it is not necessary to work your way through all the five forms of sight to produce invisibility by this method. According to Patanjali: 'Disappearance comes from *Sanyama* on the form of the body, visibility being suspended, and there being no contact with the light from the eye [of the beholder].' The 'light from the eye' is the light that we have previously discussed. 'Visibility' is the 'generic characteristic' of vision. And the 'form of the body' is the *Rupa Tanmatra* – form – applied to that which we wish to make invisible – the body.

Once again we have the idea here of acquiring power over something through its subtle aspect. Invisibility is the opposite of visibility, and visibility is understood in Yoga in a special sense – as the 'generic characteristic' of vision. We acquire power over visibility by doing *Sanyama* on the more subtle aspect of vision, which is the *Tanmatra* – form.

Now just what this means is a matter of some interpretation. Swami Vivekananda says that 'a Yogi standing in this room can apparently vanish', but he hastens to add what seems to me to be a rather artificial qualification: 'He does not really vanish, but he will not be seen by anyone. The power of perceiving forms comes from the junction of form and the thing formed. When the Yogi has attained to that power of concentration when form and the thing formed have been separated, he makes a *Sanyama* on that, and the power to perceive forms is obstructed. The form and the body are, as it were, separated.'[50]

The difficulty that Western man has in understanding this idea comes from the fact that we do not see form the way the Yogis do. We see it as a sort of abstraction. It is a convenience that we adopt in arranging our perceptions. We say that this has such-and-such a form, and that has a different form. But we do not really think of form as a *thing*. To the Yogis, form is just as real as matter. It is a stage of material development. Evans-Wentz even calls it a psychic power. He says: 'Through transcendental direction of that subtle mental faculty, or psychic power, whereby all forms, animate and inanimate, are created, the human body can be dissolved, and thereby be made invisible, by yogically inhibiting the faculty.'[51]

Alice Bailey is more explicit. In her view, 'The etheric or vital body ... functions as the attractive force holding the dense physical vehicle in shape', and 'this vital body is [therefore] the true form from the standpoint of the occultist.'[52] *Sanyama* on the form is therefore *Sanyama* on the vital body, and with that we get an insight into how this technique is performed.

Alice Bailey says that 'the soul ... withdraws itself out of the matter aspect', and that this is done 'through a concentration of [our] consciousness in the ego, the spiritual man or soul.'[53]

The Maharishi Mahesh Yogi, who teaches Patanjali's methods as a part of his TM-Sidhi Programme, tells his disciples to 'go in' so they 'don't reflect the light anymore'.[54] One of his students described the experience to Orme-Johnson as 'the body completely hiding itself, so that all that is left is the 'I-sense' (*Ahamkara*)'.[55]

In Buddhism this is said to be one of the concomitants of *Nirvana*. *Nirvana* is merely an introverted state of consciousness, in which the Adept 'goes in' as it were. If it is sufficiently perfected, the Adept 'cannot be seen by gods or men'.[56] He is invisible. Thomas Vaughan seems to speak of this in a Western context when he says that 'whosoever advances beyond the three regions passes from the sight of men'.[57] He calls this 'the stainless and oft-celebrated Invisibility of the Magi'.[58]

Just how this works is explained by Madame David-Neel in her book *Magic and Mystery in Tibet*. If you walk along through a crowd, shouting, bumping against people, and otherwise calling attention to yourself, you will make yourself quite visible. However, if you steal along noiselessly you may be able to pass without being seen.[59] Animals know this instinctively, and use it to catch their prey. As J.H. Brennan points out, merely sitting motionless cuts down on your 'visibility'. Beasts of prey avoid this difficulty by bobbing their heads, creating the illusion of 'motion'.[60]

However quiet you are, though, there is still the unquietness generated by your mind. 'The work of the mind generates an energy which spreads all around the one who produces it, and this energy is felt in various ways by those who come into touch with it.' says David-Neel. If you can stop even *that* source of noise, you become as silent as one could be. You may be 'seen' in the way that a camera 'sees' things, but you will not be noticed. 'No "knowledge-consciousness" (*nampar shespa*) follows the visual contact (*mig gi regpa*), we do not remember that this contact has taken place.'[61]

'When the mind inhibits emanation of its radioactivity,' says Evans-Wentz, 'it ceases to be the source of mental stimuli to others, so that they become unconscious of the presence of an Adept of the Art, just as they are unconscious of invisible beings living in a rate of vibration unlike their own.'[62] It is like the ostrich burying his head in the sand. One draws his attention into himself, instead of directing it outward, and by stopping the flow of the mind, turns off the noise.

In the most elementary sense, this form of 'invisibility' is just stealing along quietly. 'The real secret of invisibility is not concerned with the laws of optics at all,' writes Aleister Crowley. 'The trick is to prevent people noticing you when they would normally do so.'[63] As a test of his power, Crowley took a walk in the street 'in a golden crown and a scarlet robe without attracting attention.'[64] Eliphas Lévi makes the same point:

> A man, for example, pursued by murderers, after having run down a side street, returns instantly and comes, with a calm face, toward those who are pursuing him, or mixes with them and appears occupied with the same pursuit. He will certainly render himself invisible ... The person who would be seen is always remarked, and he who would remain unnoticed effaces himself and disappears. The will is the true Ring of Gyges.[65]

As usual, Aleister Crowley claims to have had the experience himself. He was pursued by 'a very large number of excited people' who had 'no friendly intentions; but I had a feeling of lightness, of ghostliness, as if I were a shadow moving soundlessly about the street.'[66]

The *modus operandi* here is very simple. All you must do is sit quietly, close your eyes, and allow your consciousness to slowly turn inward. No effort is required here. The turning-inward is a natural and quite involuntary process. After you feel that you have become altogether oblivious to your environment, hold in your mind the notion that you wish to 'hide', even though you may be sitting in an open room, and then eliminate all thoughts from your mind altogether.

The first part of this experiment should be quite easy for you, especially if you have ever done meditation. But the last part may not be. Stopping the noise in your head is an essential to any kind of success in life, but many people have difficulty with it, nonetheless. And only the Adepts can stop it entirely.

Yet, if the mind moves, there is motion, and motion makes you more visible. There is a way of getting around this problem, however, and it was described by J.H. Brennan as surrounding yourself with a soundproof screen.

His argument is this: if I cannot stop myself from shouting, I can conceal myself from you by surrounding myself with a soundproof screen that shuts out the noise. Likewise, if we could surround ourselves with a 'mind-proof' screen, we could shut out the noise generated by our minds.[67] There is a technique for doing that which is taught by the AMORC Rosicrucians. They call it the 'Veil of Obscurity'. It seems to me that this idea is just the logical development of Patanjali's ideas, and that it therefore should have a place here, even thought it is Western in origin.

Once again, the technique is quite simple. Sit quietly as if to meditate, close your eyes, and imagine that you are completely surrounded by just such a mind-proof screen. The Rosicrucians suggest that we think of this as a curtain, hanging down around us, and completely concealing us. You are to think of this screen until you can feel its presence, and as you do, hold in mind the idea that the screen is to make you invisible to outsiders.

If you want to check your success, it is quite simple to position a mirror in the opposite corner of the room, outside the Veil's sphere of influence. You will be able to see out, but outsiders will not be able to see in. Hence, if you are successful, your image will not appear in the mirror.

Fantastic as all this may sound, it can be done. Practice is required, and one must not expect perfect results on the first try, or even the twenty-first try. Great patience is needed to acquire occult powers. But the Maharishi Mahesh Yogi's disciples have had great success using Patanjali's methods. Invisibility has been found to be one of the more difficult *Siddhis* to acquire, but it is also one of the more rewarding.

To show you what I mean, I want to tell you next about a technique that combines invisibility with other psychic abilities. While you are learning to vanish from the sight of men, you will also be acquiring the ability to read thoughts, communication by mental power alone, and commune with spiritual beings. This last technique is called the Harpocrates god-form Assumption, and it is part of the Invisibility Ritual of the Hermetic Order of the Golden Dawn.

9. Golden Dawn Methods

We have now to consider a method that was developed in the Hermetic Order of the Golden Dawn, and which is similar in intent and practice to the 'Veil of Obscurity' experiment described in the last chapter. It is based on techniques used in ancient Egyptian magic, and is known as the Assumption of the Harpocrates god-form.

I might point out here that Assumption in various forms has been taken over from the original Golden Dawn system into later schools, and is taught in one form or another by the AMORC Rosicrucians, and also by Silva Mind Control. It is a very versatile technique, and it would not be too much to say that an ingenious student can derive all the benefits of any system of psychic culture from this one technique alone, without the benefit of any other.

It is best not to begin with the actual Assumption of Harpocrates himself, though. Assumption is best mastered in stages, beginning with simpler tasks and moving progressively on to the more difficult ones. Even in the original Golden Dawn, Dion Fortune says Assumption was 'often employed in order to enter into the inner life of a plant or a crystal as a mental exercise.'[1] This is where Silva Mind Control students begin with their Assumption experiments, and I think it best that we should start there, too.

Select, if you will, some inanimate object, preferably one that is made of a single kind of material, sit comfortably, and place the object in front of you where you can see it easily. In Silva Mind Control a

piece of copper or steel is often employed for this experiment. If you
have a crystal, you may prefer to use that. But let me suggest that it be
something simple. You wouldn't want to use, say, a Tarot card for
Assumption, at least not at first, because the complex design on the face
of the card will distract your attention. The simplicity of a crystal or a
piece of metal is closer to what you will need.

Once you have selected your object, sit quietly, close your eyes, and
visualize it in front of you. Now gradually increase the size of the
object in your visualization until it becomes quite large, large enough,
in fact, that if it were a door you could walk through it. Then imagine
that you are merging with your object, that you and the object are in
fact becoming one. Once you feel that you have been successful, and
that you have in fact merged psychically with whatever you are using,
try to become sensitive to any feelings or sensations that may come to
you. How does it feel to be a piece of steel? What does it look like? Are
there any tactile sensations that come to you? How cold is your object?
What is its texture?

If you are successful with this experiment, the first thing that will
happen is that you will actually feel that you in fact have merged with
whatever you are trying to merge with, if not physically, then
psychically. Then, as you progress with it, you will begin to have
actual sensations, intuitions, even thoughts that come to you as you do
the experiment, and which proceed directly from this sense of merging
that you will produce.

Those of you who are familiar with *Sanyama* will know that this
sense of merging often comes spontaneously to those who practise
open-eyed versions of *Sanyama*, and it is said by those who should know
that this very sense confers on the practitioner a supernormal
knowledge of, and power over, whatever he merges with. You should
not expect too much at first, but you will find with practice that this
simple technique can be developed into an instrument of great power.

After you have worked for a while with your inanimate object, it is
time to move one step up in the consciousness hierarchy and try the
same thing with a plant. You may use a tree in your front garden, or, if
you prefer, you may use the Mind Control method and pick up a leaf
somewhere. There are only two requirements: for best results you

should do the experiment with a plant that actually exists, and that is still alive. Therefore, if you use a leaf, use one that you have picked recently, and that could still be reasonably supposed to have some of the life force left in it.

Once you have selected your plant object, do the same thing that you did with the inanimate object. Place it before you, visualize it, then imagine that you are merging with it psychically. Finally, try to become sensitive to any impressions that may come to you as a result of the experiment.

Once you have worked with the plant Assumption for a while, then you may try the same thing with an animal, and finally with a human being.

In these cases, you may not be able to get the animal or the person to sit around obligingly while you try to 'assume' them. However, there should be no problem if you worked with the earlier Assumptions thoroughly enough. You will now be able to merely visualize the animal or the person standing in front of you, and then, as before, imagine that you are merging with it, so that your consciousnesses are merged together, and you become one with it.

In this case, you may wish to visualize yourself standing directly behind the person you are assuming, then, in imagination, reach out and put your hands on the sides of the other person's head. Now, imagine that you are putting his head on, in other words, that you are slipping his head over yours, just as you would a ski mask. After you have done this, try to see with his eyes, hear with his ears, and think with his brain. His thoughts will become your thoughts, and your thoughts will become his. Using this method, you can communicate with another person telepathically and implant thoughts in his mind without him being consciously aware where they came from.

Now the first time you try this, the results may be something less than extraordinary. You may have slight impressions of what the other person is thinking, which turn out to be true, or you may have an impression of what he is seeing, which will tell you where he is. Or, you may have nothing. However, the technique does work, as hundreds of people have proved, and it is one of the most useful techniques known to modern occultism. When I was in college, one of my fellow students mastered Assumption and used it to learn what his professors intended to ask in his examinations. To silence the sceptics, he would make notes on the examination content before he took it, then show the actual examination itself afterward. Others have 'assumed' inanimate objects to find out what is wrong with a piece of machinery or to learn the answers to certain chemical problems. I myself have used the technique to energize a dead car battery.

If we accept certain occult theories, the reason for all this is quite understandable. The body is composed of the dust of the earth, meaning that ultimately all the elements of which the body is composed may be found in the soil, come from the soil, and will return to it. Now this fact is generally recognized and accepted, but occultists take it one step further. They contend that there is also a consciousness-principle in man which is separate from the body and which has its own proper element. Thus, just as the body comes from the dust of the earth and returns thereto, so does the consciousness-principle in man come from a sort of consciousness-essence that pervades all space. After man dies, we would expect the consciousness-principle to return to its own proper element, just as the body returns to the dust of the earth.

Now as long as man is alive, this consciousness-principle tends to commingle with the body, yet at the same time maintaining contact with its source, just as the body is always in contact with the earth. And since this conciousness-essence on which we all depend is a conscious principle in its own right, that means that we are all tied together by a common consciousness which is impersonal, in addition to our individual consciousness-principles, which are of course personal. Other people are then different manifestations of ourselves in a certain sense, or, if you prefer, we are all different manifestations of our common consciousness-essence, the Cosmic Consciousness.

If that is true, and it is certainly an attractive idea, then it makes sense that we should each be able to become aware of our other 'identities'. In other words, I should be able, in Assumption, to become anyone else, or to become aware that I *already am* everybody else.

In *The Mansions of the Soul*, H. Spencer Lewis argued that there is a separate Oversoul for each of the kingdoms of nature. In other words, the Oversoul, or the Cosmic Consciousness, for the human kingdom is different from the Oversoul for the animal or vegetable kingdoms. However, I do not believe that to be true, and since Dr Lewis merely states this as a matter of opinion, it is impossible to criticize the reasoning by which he reached it.[2] There would appear to be one Oversoul, not only for the subhuman, but for the superhuman kingdoms as well, and that brings us to the culmination of our discussion: the Assumption of the Harpocrates god-form.

Harpocrates is, simply put, one of the deities in the ancient Egyptian pantheon. More precisely, the name Harpocrates is the Greek name for Heru-p-khart, or, as Israel Regardie spells it, Hoor-paar-Kraat.[3] There are several ways of interpreting the Harpocrates Assumption. We can assume, as the Egyptians did, that Harpocrates is a god, or we can assume that he is a personality in the Cosmic Consciousness, origin and status unknown, or we can assume, as Israel Regardie did, that he is an astral form that we build up in the Astral Light, who has no existence apart from our own conceptions of him.[4] I think this last interpretation is the most ingenious of the three, although if it is true, then technically the Harpocrates Assumption is not a true Assumption. I prefer to think of him as simply a personality who exists in the Cosmic Consciousness. But in the final analysis, the issue is unimportant. People who have tried the Harpocrates Assumption have achieved excellent results, and have left us the technique with their endorsement. That in itself makes it worth doing.

Now I might point out here that Harpocrates is, in all likelihood, a historical character. Ancient writers tell us that his father, Osiris, was a real man, who came to the primitive Egyptians from a foreign land and taught them agriculture and the rudiments of civilization. After his death, the people elevated him to the status of a god, and prayed to him, much as modern Catholics pray to the saints.[5]

In time, of course, the story of Osiris and his children, including Harpocrates, developed into legends, and then myths. A Greek writer tells us of Harpocrates that he 'is unfolded unto light from the mire, that he is seated above the lotus, that he sails in a ship, and that he changes his form every hour, according to the signs of the zodiac.'[6] This is obviously a reference to the Sun, and indeed we find in the writings of Wallis Budge mention of the fact that 'Heru-p-khrat, or

Harpocrates, was a form of the rising sun, and represented his earliest rays'.[7] Moreover, there was an esoteric side to him, because the Greek author just quoted also says of Harpocrates that 'thus, they say, *he presents himself to view*'.[8]

Those unfamiliar with Egyptian magic may be surprised to learn that the ancient Egyptians actually evoked their gods to visible appearance and in this manner learned of their habits, their mannerisms, their peculiar characteristics. Some of these evocations were suspect, of course. Eunapius says of Iamblichus that he was present at such a ceremony designed to evoke the image of the god Apollo. The spectre did not fail to appear, arrayed in full battle armour, but the philosopher was unimpressed. He turned to one of his disciples and explained that it was merely the shade of a dead gladiator.[9]

In his book *On the Mysteries*, Iamblichus outlines a detailed system for testing such appearances, to determine the rank of the spirit that has been evoked.[10] It was in this manner that the paintings of Harpocrates that are found in Egyptian frescoes were done, and it is on that basis that we shall use the postures shown in these for our Assumption.

Referring to the myth of Harpocrates, Iamblichus admits that 'all superior natures rejoice in the similitude to themselves of inferior beings', meaning that he thought Harpocrates to be human in form. But he seems to consider much of the attendant imagery to be esoteric symbolism, or, as he puts it, 'certain images exhibited through symbols of mystic, occult, and invisible intellections'.[11]

By 'mire' he says we are to understand 'the primordial cause of the elements, and of all the powers distributed about the elements, which must be antecedently conceived to exist analogous to a foundation.'[12] Harpocrates is therefore 'the god who is the cause of all generation, of all nature, and of all the powers in the elements', and as such he 'precedes all things and comprehends all things in himself'. Because 'he comprehends all things and imparts himself to all mundane natures, he is from these *unfolded into light*'.

Now this is what Damascius meant when he said that 'of the first principles … the Egyptians said nothing, but celebrated it as a darkness beyond all intellectual comprehension, a thrice unknown darkness.'[13] The alchemists symbolized this darkness with the blackness of putrefaction, which they described as 'a blackness blacker than back itself'.[14] Flamel makes it quite clear that this blackness also referred to the *cloud*, because he says that 'this blackness is (esoterically) called "the head of the crow" ', and he explains that 'when the *Cloud* appears no more, this body is said to be without a head'. That is to say, the blackness has disappeared with it.[15] Harpocrates' emergence from mire into the light therefore refers to the formation of the Worlds from out of the *cloud* at the time of the Creation, and herein lies the importance of the Harpocrates Assumption in invisibility. Whenever Harpocrates is visualized in Assumption, he is visualized as surrounded with the darkness of the *cloud*.[16] Thus, by assuming the Harpocrates god-form, we are doing much the same thing as we do when we form the 'Veil of Obscurity'. That is, we imagine that the condition we want is surrounding our bodies and shutting out the light, only in this case we do it as part of a larger exercise. Now let us look at the rest of the symbolism:

'Because he transcends all things, and is by himself expanded above them,' says Iamblichus, 'on this account he presents himself to the view as separate, exempt, elevated, and expanded by himself above the powers and elements of the world. The following symbol testifies the truth of this. For by the god "*sitting above the lotus*" a transcendency and strength which by no means come into contact with the mire are obscurely signified, and also indicate his intellectual and empyrean empire. For everything belonging to the lotus is seen to be circular, *viz.* both the form of the leaves and the fruit; and circulation is alone allied to the motion of the intellect, which energizes with invariable sameness, in one order, and according to reason. But the god is established by himself, and above a dominion and energy of this kind, venerable and holy, superexpanded, and abiding in himself, which his being seated is intended to signify. When the god, also, is represented as "*sailing in a ship*", it exhibits to us the power which governs the world. As, therefore, the pilot being separate from the ship presides over the rudder of it, thus the sun having a separate subsistence, governs the helm of the whole world. And as the pilot directs all things from the stern, giving from himself a small principle of motion to the vessel; thus, also, by a much greater priority, the god indivisibly imparts supernally from the first principles of nature, the primordial causes of motions.'[17]

To do the Harpocrates Assumption, first read and re-read the descriptions of the god and the symbolism connected with him, until you feel that you have thoroughly assimilated their meaning. Meditate on Harpocrates, visualize him energing from the primordial darkness, and think about him until he becomes real to you. There is an unmistakable sensation that will come to you when you have succeeded with this. When you feel that you have succeeded, stand up, place your right foot in front of your left and about six inches to the right of it, and bring your right forefinger to your lips in the traditional Sign of Silence. Imagine that you are in fact becoming the god Harpocrates, that your personality is merging with his, and as you do this, vibrate the name *Hoor-po-krat-ist*, while imagining that you are emerging from primeval waters, with the lotus blossom at your feet.

This may all seem rather complicated, but in practice it is quite easy. There are several distinct steps here: learning about the legends and myths surrounding the god, until you feel that you 'know' him as well as if he were one of your friends; building up a mental image of the god until you can almost sense his presence; assuming the posture traditionally associated with him; and finally, performing the Assumption itself.

There is an affirmation that you might wish to employ here to heighten the effect of the visualizations just described. It comes from one of the Golden Dawn manuscripts and consists of two parts: an invocation of Harpocrates, and an affirmation that you and he have become one:

Hoor-po-krat-ist, Thou Lord of the Silence, Hoor-po-krat-ist, Lord of the Sacred Lotus, O Thou Hoor-po-krat-ist [*pause a moment or two to contemplate the force invoked*], Thou that standest in victory on the heads of the infernal dwellers of the waters wherefrom all things were created, Thee, Thee, I invoke, by the name of *Eheieh* and the power of *Agla*.

Behild! He is in me, and I in him. Mine is the Lotus as I rise as Harpocrates from the firmament of waters ... For I am Hoor-po-krat-ist, the Lotus-throned Lord of Silence … I am Ra enshrouded, Khephra unmanifest to man.[18]

If you are successful, and I mean successful in an advanced sense, you will be able to see through the eyes and hear with the ears of Harpocrates, just as with less advanced forms of Assumption you learn to see with the eyes and hear with the ears of some other mortal. And since Harpocrates looks out upon heavenly scenes and listens to celestial music, you will find that you have acquired the secret of the Ascension into Heaven, described in Chapter Two. It is because of this that another word for Ascension is Assumption.

Now I do not wish to infer that just anybody can do this experiment once or twice and experience the Ascension. That is one of the more advanced experiences that may come to you after you have been working with this exercise for some time; however, it is common enough that there is a mention of it in the Golden Dawn manuscripts. 'Divine ecstasy may follow.' says one manuscript, 'but guard against loss of self-control.'[19]

Another possible effect for advanced students of Assumption is that the Shroud of Concealment, 'the blue-black egg of Harpocrates', as the G.D. manuscripts call it, will begin to form around you and conceal you from the sight of men.[20] You will remember from Chapter Two that such manifestations are usually mentioned as accompanying the purely spiritual experiences in detailed descriptions of Ascensions into Heaven. 'The effect should be that the physical body will become gradually and partially invisible, as though a *veil* or *cloud* were coming between it and Thee.'[21]

Aleister Crowley actually tried this experiment during a visit to Mexico and described his results in his *Confessions*. 'I reached a point where my physical reflection in a mirror became faint and flickering,' he wrote. 'It gave very much the effect of the interrupted images of the cinematograph in its early days.'[22] The cloud forms during the Harpocrates Assumption because Harpocrates himself is said to be surrounded by the cloud. As for the reference to the 'blue-black egg', we must remember that the cloud is concentrated *Akasa*, and *Akasa* is space.[23]

Somehow it does not seem to me that blue-black should be the proper colour of space, but it does to other people. In *The Magus*, for example, John Fowler speaks of 'the blue-black breath of space'. The egg is simply the shape of the human aura.

When we do the Harpocrates Assumption, after assuming the identity of Harpocrates, we imagine that the blue-black egg is forming around us, just as it is said to be formed around the god. In fact, the Golden Dawn manuscripts use more forceful language than the word 'imagine'. 'Project your whole Will so as to realize the self fading out', we are told.[24] 'Formulate forcibly the egg of dark blue-black.'[25] 'Formulate shroud forcibly.'[26] 'Intensely formulate Shroud.'[27] We must do what we do in the Veil of Obscurity experiment — mentally formulate a condition of some kind surrounding ourselves which will block out light. In fact, this *is* the Veil of Obscurity experiment, with the addition of the Harpocrates god-form Assumption to enhance the effect.

It is also the core of the 'Ritual of Invisibility' as taught by the Hermetic Order of the Golden Dawn. I am not going to give the complete text of this ritual because it needs to be studied in connection with the whole system of Golden Dawn magic. Those who are interested in it are encouraged to get Israel Regardie's *The Golden Dawn*, (published by Llewellyn Publications and distributed in Britain by The Aquarian Press). However, I should like to outline the system of techniques that it comprises.

We are told to open with the Lesser Banishing Rituals of the Pentagram *and* the Hexagram.[28] This is to be followed with an 'Enochian Spirit Invocation', which is *also* a banishing ritual, and *that* banishing is followed in turn by the Harpocrates Assumption, which is considered a banishing ritual as well.[29] That seems to be to be quite a lot of banishing, and if it is necessary to cut down on the length of the ritual, you might find that here is the place to do it. Do the Lesser Banishing Ritual of the Pentagram if you are so inclined, but the rest seems hardly necessary.

After all of this banishing, we are told to do some *evoking*. Evoking is just summoning. Whereas with banishing we try to get rid of any spirits that might be in the vicinity, in evoking, we ask the spirits to come. The idea is naturally to enlist the aid of any Beings who might command more magical power than we do, and whereas we might think such Beings too majestic to answer the cries of a mere mortal, *The Key of Solomon* assures us 'they *will* come, even if they be bound with chains of fire'.[30]

This is a very old idea in ceremonial magic. *The Key of Solomon* itself contains such conjurations: 'Abac, Aldal, Iat, Hudac, Guthac, Guthor, Gomeh, Tistator, Derisor, Destatur, come hither all he who love the times and places wherein all kinds of mockeries are practiced.'[31] And in another place:

> Sceaboles, Arbaron, Elohi, Elimigith, Herenobulcule, Methe, Baluth, Timayal, Villaquiel, Teveni, Yevie, Ferete, Bacuhaba, Guvarin; through Him through Whom ye have empire and power over men, ye must accomplish this work so that I may go and remain invisible.
>
> O thou Almiras, Master of Invisibility, with thy Ministers Cheros, Maitor, Tangedem, Transidim, Suvantos, Abelaios, Bored, Belamith, Castumi, Dabuel; I conjure ye by Him Who maketh Earth and Heaven to tremble, Who is seated upon the throne of His majesty, that this operation may be perfectly accomplished according to my will, so that at whatsoever time it may please me, I may be able to be invisible.[32]

The actual names of the spirits invoked do not seem to be very important. *The Key of Solomon* itself contains four different lists of names, and there are others, entirely different, in other books.

Grillot de Givry, for example, quotes a long Latin conjuration from *Le Secret des secrets*, a manuscript in the Bibliothèque de l'Arsenal in Paris. The only name that is mentioned twice — and long strings of names are recited twice before the conjuration is finished — is that of the Master Pontation, who apparently rules all the inferior spirits.[33] Still other names may be found in *The Book of the Sacred Magic of Abra-Merlin the Mage*.[34]

For that reason, this particular aspect of Golden Dawn magic is not really to my taste. As Israel Regardie so astutely observed, 'you can be a highly religious person or an atheist. It does not interfere with the practice of Yoga.' But 'Magic is a good deal different ... Magic does require faith in some religious hierarchy ... It is difficult to intone and vibrate invocations or prayers when you know you are a thoroughgoing hypocrite to address these invocations to someone or something whose very being you deny.'[35] To evoke the spirits, you must *believe* in the spirits. At the very least there must be a suspension of dis-belief. And that I find difficult to pull off. I have little difficulty accepting the possible existence of Harpocrates for the purpose of Assumption. But I find it difficult to believe in Methe, Bored, Dabuel, and the Master Pontation. That is why I prefer to work with the non-magical yoga-based systems. Each to his own taste.

There are other techniques comprised within the Golden Dawn ritual that do not require this belief in spirits, however. One of these is to address your invocations and evocations directly to the astral matter of the cloud itself. Now you must believe in *that*, or else you would not commence the experiment in the first place. And by using an evocation, you may direct the full force of your will toward it.

Most of the commands addressed directly toward the cloud take this form:

> Come to me, O shroud of darkness and of night, by the power of the name Yeheshuah, Yehovashah. Formulate about me, thou divine egg of the darkness of spirit. I conjure ye, O particles of astral darkness, that ye enfold me as a guard and shroud of utter silence and of mystery.
>
> I conjure and invoke this shroud of concealment ... I invoke ye and conjure ye. I evoke ye potently. I command and constrain ye. I compel ye to absolute, instant, and complete obedience, and that without deception and delay ... And I declare that with the divine Aid in this Operation I *shall* succeed, that the Shroud *shall* conceal me alike from men and spirits, that it *shall* be under my control, ready to disperse and to re-form at my command.[36]

In some places this is connected with a portion of a rhyme – I hesitate to say poem – that for some reason never quite rhymes. I suspect there may be some magical reason for using an incomplete rhyme, but here is what appears to be the *complete* rhyme, reconstructed from the several fragments:

> Gather, ye flakes of Astral Light
> To shroud my form in your substantial Night;
> Clothe me, and hide me, but at my control,
> Darken men's eyes, and blind their souls;
> Gather, O gather, at my word divine,
> For ye are the Watchers, my soul is the shrine.[37]

This little rhyme does have considerable power over the imagination when recited with feeling, and some of you may find it useful in your experiments.

Another Golden Dawn technique involves evoking the power of the Sephiroth *Binah*. Binah is one of the Ten Sephiroth on the Qabalistic Tree of Life. It is the third in the series, and is connected with all sorts of attributions that suggest *invisibility*. According to the *Book of the Path of the Chameleon* — one of the Golden Dawn manuscripts — 'in *Binah* is a *thick darkness*, which yet veileth the Divine Glory in which all colours are hidden, wherein is mystery and depth and silence.'[38] In a fragment of *The Key of Solomon*, given by Eliphas Lévi in his *Philosophe Occulte*, we are told that the Qlippoth of *Binah* are '*Satariel, the concealers*'.[39] The Archangel is *Tzaphqiel*, derived from the Hebrew TzPH, meaning 'a covering or shroud'.[40] And the 'Sphere of its Operation is *Shabbathai*', the planet Saturn in the outer world, which gives forms and similitudes unto chaotic matter' — the substance of the *cloud*.[41]

The invocations to *Binah* are addressed as if to a person, which is as we would expect, since MacGregor Mathers seems to have considered all of the Qabalistic Spheres to represent personified entities. Thus we are told to say things like this:

> O ye strong and mighty ones of the Sphere of Shabbathai, ye Aralim, I conjure ye by the mighty name of Yhvh Elohim, the divine ruler of Binah, and by the name of Tzaphqiel, your Archangel. Aid me with your power, in your office to place a *veil*

between me and all things belonging to the outer and material world. Clothe me with a *veil* woven from that silent darkness which surrounds your abode of eternal rest in the Sphere of Shabbathai.[42]

After you have succeeded – and a certain amount of practice will be necessary for success – you are to perform another simple ritual to disintegrate the shroud and banish it until it is needed again. This is a point that is unique to the Golden Dawn system. The AMORC Rosicrucians do not suggest that one 'banishes' the cloud after using it, and neither do any of the other groups experimenting with invisibility. But the Golden Dawn manuscripts insist that 'on no account must that shroud of awful Mystery be left without disintegration, seeing that it would speedily attract an occupant which would become a terrible vampire preying upon him who had called it into being'. We are therefore told to 'rehearse a conjuration as aforesaid, and then open the Shroud and come forth out of the midst thereof, and then disintegrate that shroud by the use of a conjuration unto the forces of *Binah*.'[43] The conjuration is quite simple:

> In the name of Yhvh Elohim, I invoke thee, who art clothed with the Sun, who standest upon the Moon, and art crowned with the crown of twelve stars. Aima Elohim, Shekinah, Who art Darkness illuminated by the Light divine, send me thine Archangel Tzaphqiel, and thy legions of Aralim, the might Angels of the Sphere of Shabbathai, that I may disintegrate and scatter this shroud of darkness and of mystery, for its work is ended for the hour.
>
> I conjure Thee, O shroud of darkness and of Mystery, which has well served my purpose, that thou now depart unto thine ancient ways. But be ye, whether by word or will, or by this great invocation of your powers, ready to come quickly and forcibly to my behest, again to shroud me from the eyes of men. And now I say unto ye, Depart in peace, with the blessing of God the Vast and Shrouded One, and be ye very ready to come when ye are called.[44]

This conjuration is followed by the Lesser Banishing Rituals of the Pentagram and the Hexagram, which give added force to the spoken word.

Whether this is really necessary is, of course, problematical. As I have said, the Harpocrates Assumption is considered to be a banishing ritual in itself. And in *The Tree of Life*, speaking of the Harpocrates Assumption, Israel Regardie says that 'the surrounding of the astral body with the egg of blue-black or indigo is sufficiently powerful to banish any unwanted influence, inasmuch as it elevates the Magician above that realm.'[45] Nonetheless, there are differences of opinion.

It has been noted that anyone surrounded with the cloud feels a sensation of coolness. In his *History of Spiritualism*, Conan Doyle compares this with 'the cold chill, the sudden faint' that some people report who have seen a ghost. He believes that this feeling is due not to terror but to vampirism.[46] The cloud literally absorbs vital energy from the person who is closest to it.

Now that is not so surprising, since, as we have seen, it is formed originally from someone's vital energy. But since the cloud is used whenever a projected astral entity wishes to make himself manifest, it is not inconceivable that an entity, wishing to manifest, might make use of a cloud formed by someone on the earth plane for the purpose. I have never had any such experience, but others have.

In his *Paracelsus*, Franz Hartmann tells of a young man who killed himself on account of his passion for a married woman: 'The latter loved him, but did not encourage his advances on account of her matrimonial obligations. After his death, his astral form became attracted to her, and as she was of a mediumistic temperament, he found the necessary conditions to become partially materialized.'[47]

This is what is known as an Incubus. It is not altogether unknown where suicides are concerned, especially if they terminate a love affair. Hartmann says that 'they cannot become visible unless they can draw some of the astral essence from the person in whose presence they desire to appear.'[48] When this happens spontaneously, 'there must be some fault in the organization [of the medium], else the combination of their principles would be too strong to part with some of their astral substance.'[49] Uncontrolled mediumship, he says, 'may prove to be very injurious in the end.'[50] And, in a particularly weird note, he says that 'Chinamen and Hindus have been known to kill themselves for the purpose of revenge, so that their souls may cling to their enemies and trouble their minds or drive them to suicide ... Wars are often followed by numerous suicides in the victorious army.'[51]

The theory behind this is that each of us has an appointed time to die. The Pearly Gates will not open for us until our time has come. And when we die before our time, either because of suicide or untimely accident, we must walk the earth until the proper moment has arrived.[52] In *The Tibetan Book of the Dead* these earthbound spiritis are known as *pretas* — 'unhappy ghosts'.[53] An existence as a *preta* is considered one of six possible fates that may await a departed soul, the best being sojourn in one of the Heaven-Worlds, and the worst being condemnation to one of the Hells.[54] If you know anyone who has committed suicide, if you have a mediumistic temperament, or if you have experimented in evocations of spirits, evil or otherwise, you might wish to consider using such a banishing ritual. Most people can simply leave it off without ill effect.

Notes

Chapter 1:

1. Gabriel Naude, *Instruction à la France sur la verité de l'histoire Frères de la Roze-Croiz*. Paris: Chevallier, 1624, p. 26.

2. Charles Mackay, LL.D. *Extraordinary Popular Delusions and the Madness of Crowds*. London: Richard Bentley, 1841. For the original French text of the proclamation, see Naude, p. 27, and *Mercure François*, p. 371.

3. *La Neufiesme tome du Mercure François, ou, suite de l'histoire de nostre temps*. Paris, 1624. It was from this source that Mackay evidently got most of his information.

4. Mackay, op. cit.

5. *Mercure François*, p. 371.

6. Mackay, op. cit. See also *Mercure François*, pp. 372-4.

7. Naude, op. cit.

8. Neuhusius, *Advertissement pieux et très utile des Frères de la R. C.* Paris, 1624, p. 115.

9. 'A Gossip About the Rosicrucians', *Chambers' Edinburgh Journal*, 1886, vol. 6, pp. 298-316.

10. Robert F. Gould, *History of Freemasonry*. Cincinnati: J.C. Yorston & Co., 1884-1889, vol. 3, p. 191.

11. John Aubrey, *Three Prose Works*, edited by J .B. Brown. Southern Illinois University Press, 1972, p. 253.

12. Frances Barrett, *The Magus*. Secaucus, New Jersey: The Citadel Press, 1975, p. 40. Available from the Aquarian Press.

13. Ben Jonson, *The Vnderwood*, in *The poems, the Prose Works*. Oxford University Press, 1947, vol. 8, p. 206.

14. Lord Bulwer-Lytton, *Zanoni, a Rosicrucian Tale*, Blauvelt, New York:

Rudolph Steiner Publications, 1971, p. 218.

15. Wynn Westcott, quoted by Ellic Howe, *The Magicians of the Golden Dawn*. London: Routledge & Kegan Paul, 1972, p. 31.

16. Letter to Hargrave Jennings, quoted by Paul Allen in the preface to Lytton's *Zanoni*, p. 4.

17. H. Spencer-Lewis, *The Mystical Life of Jesus*. The Supreme Grand Lodge, AMORC, Inc., 1971, p. 285.

18. H. Spencer-Lewis, *The Secret Doctrines of Jesus*. The Supreme Grand Lodge, AMORC, Inc., 1967, p. 146.

19. *The Life of Edward Bulwer, First Lord Lytton, By His Grandson, Earl of Lytton*. London: Macmillan, 1913, vol. 2, p. 40.

20. *Confessio Fraternitatis Rosae Crucis*, in Paul Allen's *Christian Rosenkreutz Anthology*. Blauvelt, New York: Rudolph Steiner Publications, 1968, p. 184. The translation contained therein is from Thomas Vaughn's 1652 edition.

21. 'The Invisible Magic Mountain', translated by Kenneth Mackenzie. Appeared in *The Rosicrucian*, London, 1875. Another version translated by Thomas Vaughan appeared in *Lumen de Lumine*.

22. Thomas Vaughan, *The Works of Thomas Vaughan*, edited by Arthur Edward Waite. New Hyde Park, New York: University Books, 1968, p. 354.

23. Israel Regardie, *The Golden Dawn*. Saint Paul, Minnesota: Llewellyn Publications, 1971, vol. 3, book 6, p. 237.

24. Franz Hartmann, *The Life and the Doctrines of Philippus Theophrastus, Bombast of Hohenheim, Known by the Name of Paracelsus*. New York: United States Book Company, 191, pp. 345-6.

25. 'Invisibility', in *Hastings' Encyclopedia of Religion and Ethics*.

26. Edward Conze, *Buddhist Scriptures*. Baltimore: Penguin Books, 1959, p. 124.

27. S.L. MacGregor Mathers, *The Book of the Sacred Magic of Abra-Melin the Mage*. New York: Dover, 1975, pp. 200-201.

28. King James I, *Demonologie*. Edinburgh, 1597.

29. 'The Famous History of Friar Bacon', in *Some Old English Worthies*, edited by Dorothy Senior. London: Stephen Swift & Co., 1952, pp. 223-5.

Chapter 2:

1. *The Odyssey of Homer*, translated by S.H. Butcher and Andrew Lang. New York: P.F. Collier & Son, 1909, p. 79.

2. *Ibid.*, p.80.

3. *Ibid.*, p. 82.

4. *The Odyssey*, translated by Samuel Butler. New York: W.J. Black, 1944, pp. 95-97.

5. 'Invisibility', in *Hastings' Encyclopedia of Religion and Ethics*.

6. *The Illiad*, translated by Samuel Butler. New York: W.J. Black, 1942, p. 220.

7. *Hesiod*, translated by Richmond Lattimore. Ann Arbor, Michigan: The University of Michigan Press, 1959, p. 33.

8. Sigmund Freud, *Moses and Monotheism*, translated by Katherine Jones. New York: A.A. Knopf, 1939.

9. Josephus, *Antiquities of the Jews*, translated by William Whiston. Grand Rapids, Michigan: Kregel Publishing Company, 1971, p. 103.

10. 'Cloud', in *The Jewish Encyclopedia*. Ktav Publishing House, undated, vol. 4, p. 122.

11. Doane, *Bible Myths and Their Parallels in Other Religions*. New Hyde Park, New York: University Books, 1971.

12. *Acts* 1.9, quoted by Doane.

13. H. Spencer-Lewis, *The Secret Doctrines of Jesus*, p. 146.

14. Olivier Leroy, *Levitation*. London: B. Oates & Washbourne, 1928, p. 180.

15. Apollodorus, *The Library*, translated by Sir James George Fraser. London: The Loeb Classical Library, 1921, vol. 1, p. 271.

16. *Ibid.*

17. II Kings 2:1-11.

18. Richard Maurice Bucke, *Cosmic Consciousness*. Philadelphia: Innes & Sons, 1902.

19. *Ibid.*

20. Lee Sannella, *Kundalini – Psychosis or Transcendence?* San Francisco: H.S. Dakin Co., 1977.

21. *The Secret of the Golden Flower*, translated by Richard Wilhelm. New York: Causeway Books, 1975, p. 56.

22. *Ibid.*

23. Cornelius Agrippa, quoted by Thomas Vaughan in *Works*, p. 107.

24. Dante, *La Vita Nuova*, quoted by Lotus Dudley in *Le Comte de Gabalis*. London, 1922.

25. *Ibid.*, note 10.

26. D.H. Rawcliffe, *Occult and Supernatural Phenomena*. New York: Dover, 1959.

27. H.P. Blavatsky, *Isis Unveiled*. Los Angeles, California: The Theosophy Company, 1968, vol. 2, p. 596.

28. Trowbridge, *Cagliostro*. New Hyde Park, New York: University Books, undated, p. 207.

29. H. Spencer Lewis, *The Rosicrucian Manual*. San Jose, California: The Rosicrucian Press, Ltd., 1966, p. 169.

30. Dionysius of Halicarnassus, *Roman Antiquities*, translated by Edward Spelman. London, 1758, vol. 1, pp. 176-7.

31. H.P. Blavatsky, *Isis Unveiled*, vol. 2, pp. 104-5.

32. Sir Arthur Conan Doyle, *The History of Spiritualism*. New York: Arno Press, 1975, p. 106.

33. *Ibid.*

34. Charles Richet, *Thirty Years of Psychic Research*, translated by Stanley de Broth. New York: Macmillan, 1923, pp. 469, 470, 499.

35. *Ibid.*, p. 478.

36. Augustine, *City of God*, translated by George E. McCracken. London: The Loeb Classical Library, 1957.

37. H.P. Blavatsky, *Isis Unveiled*, vol. 2, pp. 609-610.

38. Manly P. Hall, *An Encyclopedic Outline of Masonic, Hermetic, Qabbalistic and Rosicrucian Symbolical Philosophy*. Los Angeles: The Philosophical Research Society, Inc., 1973, p. cx.

39. H.P. Blavatsky, *Isis Unveiled*, vol. 1, p. 476.

40. W.B. Yeats, *Autobiographies*. New York: Macmillan and Company, 1953, p. 122.

41. Hartmann, *Paracelsus*, p. 346.

42. *Ibid.*, p. 290n.

Chapter 3:

1. Paul M. Allen and Carlo Pietzner, *A Christian Rosenkreutz Anthology*. Blauvelt, New York: Rudolph Steiner Publications, 1968, p. 287.

2. Hermes Trismegistus, *The Book of Seven Chapters*, otherwise known as *The Golden Treatise of Hermes Trismegistus*. Complete text in M.A. Atwood, *A Suggestive Inquiry into the Hermetic Mystery*. London: Trelawney Saunders, 1850.

3. Quoted by Arthur Edward Waite, *The Real History of the Rosicrucians*. Blauvelt, New York: Rudolph Steiner Publications, 1977, p.277. The original German text may be found in Will-Erich Peuckert's *Das Rosenkreutz*. Berlin: Erich Schmidt Verlag, 1973, pp. 339-350.

4. Dr. John Dee, *A Treatise of the Rosie-Crucian Secrets*, unpublished

manuscript in the British Museum, Harleian collection, 6485.

5. Nicolas Flamel, *Hieroglyphical Figures*. London: T.S. for Thomas Walsley at the Eagle and Child in Britain's Bursse, 1624, p. 37.

6. Hermes, op. cit.

7. Flamel, p. 37.

8. Euxodus, *The Six Keys*. Complete text in Atwood, op. cit.

9. Allen and Pietzner, p. 247. All translations made from the original German text.

10. *The Hermetic Museum*, edited by A.E. Waite, translator unknown. New York: Samuel Weiser, 1973, vol. 1, p. 27.

11. Eirenaeus Philalethes, *The Marrow of Alchemy*, in Atwood, op. cit.

12. Bloomfield, *Camp of Philosophy*, in Atwood. Originally taken from Elias Ashmole's *Theatrum Chemicum Britannicum*. London, 1652.

13. Carl Jung, *Psychology and Alchemy*, translated by F.C. Hull. Princeton, New Jersey: Princeton University Press, 1968, p. 229.

14. Thomas Vaughan, *Coelum Terrae*, in *The Works of Thomas Vaughan, Mystic and Alchemist*, collected from originals in the British Museum and annotated by Arthurd Edward Waite. New Hyde Park, New York: University Books, 1968.

15. Dom Pernety, *The Great Art*, translated by Edouard Blitz. New York: Samuel Weiser, 1973, p. 81.

16. Arthur Edward Waite, *Alchemists Through the Ages*. Blauvelt, New York: 1970, pp. 40-1. The quotation from Ripley is originally from *The Twelve Gates of Alchemy*, in Ashmole, op. cit., p. 116.

17. Franz Hartmann, *The Life and the Doctrines of Philippus Theophrastus, Bombast of Hohenheim, known by the name of Paracelsus* ... Boston: United States Book Company, 1891.

18. Morien Romanus, *A Testament of Alchemy, Being the Revelations of Morien, Ancient Adept and Hermit of Jerusalem* ... translated by Leo Stavenhagen. Hanover, New Hampshire: The University Press of New England, 1974, pp. 41, 45, 47.

19. Pernety, p. 81.

20. Atwood, op. cit.

21. Bernard Jaffee, *Crucibles*. New York: Simon and Schuster, 1930, p. 2.

22. Atwood, op. cit.

23. Hermes, *The Book of the Seven Chapters*.

24. Pernety, pp. 75-6.

25. Pernety, p. 57.

26. *The Siva Samhita*, translated by Srisachandra Vasu. Allahabad, 1914, p. 11.

27. Maharishi Maresh Yogi, *On the Bhagavad-Gita*, New York: Penguin Books, 1976, p. 479.

28. Aleister Crowley, *Eight Lectures on Yoga*. Dallas: Sangreal Foundation, Inc., 1972, p. 59. The same idea was anticipated by Hartmann, who in *Paracelsus* said: 'forms are, so to say, *crystallized space*', p. 262.

29. Quoted by Joseph Jastrow in *Wish and Wisdom*. New York: D. Appleton-Century Co., Inc., 1935, p. 354.

30. C.W. Leadbeater, *Man Visible and Invisible*. London: The Theosophical Publishing House, 1971, p. 73.

31. H. Spencer Lewis, *The Rosicrucian Manual*. San Jose, California: Rosicrucian Press, Ltd., 1966, p. 167.

32. *Ibid.*

Chapter 4:

1. Branko D. Popovic, *Introductory Engineering Electromagnetics*. Reading, Massachusetts: Addison-Wesley, 1971, pp. 23, 245.

2. *Ibid.*, p. 309.

3. *Ibid.*, p. 91.

4. J.H. Brennan, *Astral Doorways*. London: The Aquarian Press Ltd., 1971, pp. 112-113.

5. *Ibid.*

6. Popovic, p. 515.

7. J.H. Brennan, *Experimental Magic*. London: The Aquarian Press Ltd., 1972, p. 112.

8. Reginald Scott, *The Discoverie of Witchcraft*. London, 1651, book xv.

9. J.H. Brennan, *Experimental Magic*, p. 112.

Chapter 5:

1. Pliny, *Natural History*. London: The Loeb Classical Library, 1958-1963, book 7, chapter 21.

2. Mann, et. al., *Introduction to Psychology*. Boston: Houghton Mifflin, & Co., 1969, pp. 134, 136.

3. Harris Grumman, *New Ways to Better Sight*. New York: Heritage House, 1950, p. 177.

4. Lawrence Galton, 'Improve Your Sight Without Glasses', *Coronet*, October, 1955, pp. 170-1.

5. Aldous Huxley, *The Art of Seeing*. London: Harper & Brothers, 1942.

6. *Ibid.*, p. 45.

7. Lyall Watson, *The Romeo Error*. New York: Dell Publishing Company, 1976, p. 136.

8. Martin Gardner, *Fads and Fallacies*. New York: Dover, 1957, p. 232. This book was written by a hostile witness; nonetheless, it contains a very good article on Bates.

9. *Ibid.*

10. Huxley, p. 172.

11. *Ibid.*, p. 178.

12. Arthur Edward Waite, *The Mysteries of Magic*. London: George Redway, 1886, p. 348.

13. Quoted by Edwin Babbitt, *The Principles of Light and Colour*. New York: Babbitt & Co., 1878.

14. Grumman, p. 184.

15. Huxley, p. 88.

16. *Ibid.*, p. 87.

17. Babbitt, p. 549.

18. *Ibid.*, p. 550.

19. Waite, *Mysteries*, p. 346.

20. Rama Prasad, *Nature's Finer Forces*. Adyar, Madras, India: The Theosophical Publishing House, 1933.

21. Peggy Taylor and Rick Ingrasci, 'Kundalini Casualties; A *New Age* Interview with Itzhak Bentov', *New Age*, March 1978, pp. 41 seq.

22. H.P. Blavatsky, *An Abridgement of the Secret Doctrine*, edited by Elizabeth Preston and Christmas Humphreys. London: The Theosophical Publishing House, 1968. The same observation may be found in Conan Doyle's *History of Spiritualism* and Hartmann's *Paracelsus*.

23. Quoted by Lee Sannella, *Kundalini — Psychosis or Transcendence?* San Francisco: H. Dakin Co., 1977.

24. Olcott, *Old Diary Leaves*. New York and London: G.P. Putnam's Sons, 1895.

25. *Ibid.*

26. *Yoga Sutras*, Book 3, Sutra 41.

27. W.Y. Evans-Wentz, *Tibetan Yoga and Secret Doctrines*. London: Oxford University Press, 1977, pp. 172 et seq.

28. R.M. Bucke, *Cosmic Consciousness* .

29. W.J, Kilner, *The Human Atmosphere*. New York and London: Rebman

Company, 1911.

30. W.E. Butler, *How to Read the Aura*. Aquarian Press, 1979.

31. Flo Conway and Jim Siegelman, *Snapping*. New York: J.B. Lippincott, 1978, p. 174.

Chapter 6

1. Emile Grillot de Givry, *Illustrated Anthology of Sorcery, Magic, and Alchemy*. New York: Causeway Books, 1973, p. 185.

2. Albertus Magnus, *The Book of Secrets*. Oxford University Press, 1973, pp. 26-7.

3. Richard Cavendish, *The Black Art*. New York: G.P. Putnam, 1980, pp. 277-8. See also Aubrey, *Three Prose Works*, pp. 236-7.

4. Aubrey, op. cit., p. 237.

5. Benjamin Jowett, *The Works of Plato*. New York: Tudor Publishing Company, undated, pp. 47-8.

6. *Ibid.*, p. 48

7. *Ibid.*, p. 46.

8. Reginald Scot, *Discoverie of Witchcraft*, book xv.

9. *Alchemy, Religion, and Medicine in the China of A.D. 320*, translated by James Ware, The M.I.T. Press, 1966, p. 251.

10. E.A.W. Budge, *Amulets and Talismans*. New York: University Books, 1961, p. 311.

11. *The Book of the Sacred Magic of Abra-Melin the Mage*, Aquarian Press, 1980, p. 147.

12. Reginald Scot, op. cit., book xv. Scot identified the Spaniards as John Jauregui, 'servant to Gasper Anastro' and he invites us to 'read the whole discourse hereof printed at London for Tho: Chard and Will: Brome booksellers.' I have been unable to trace the original on so scant a reference.

13. Grillot de Givry, op. cit., p. 185.

14. Albertus Magnus, op. cit., pp. 41, 99.

15. *Ibid.*

16. Quoted by Crowley, *Eight Lectures on Yoga*, p. 68.

17. Eliphas Lévi, *Dogme et Rituel de la Haute Magie*. Paris: Editions Bussiere, 1977, pp. 276-7.

18. Olcott, *Old Diary Leaves*, p. 22n.

19. *Ibid.*, pp. 46-7.

20. *Ibid.*, pp. 22-3.

21. *Ibid.*, p. 47.

22. Quoted by Sprenger, *Malleus Maleficarum*, translated by Montague Summers.

23. *Ibid.*

24. F.L. Marcuse, *Hypnosis, Fact and Fiction*. Baltimore: Penguin Books, 1959, pp. 72-3.

25. Quoted by Charles Baudouin, *Suggestion and Autosuggestion*. New York: Dodd, Mead & Co., 1922, p. 238.

26. H. Laurence Shaw, *Hypnosis in Practice*. London: Balliere Tindall, 1977, p. 47.

27. Quoted by Boris Sidis, M.A., PhD., *Psychology of Suggestion*. New York and London: D. Appleton & Co., 1921, pp. 109 et seq.

28. Quoted by Doane, *Bible Myths*.

29. *Ibid.*

30. Israel Regardie, *The Tree of Life*. New York: Samuel Weiser, 1978, p. 94. Available from The Aquarian Press.

31. Long John Nebel, *The Way Out World*. Englewood Cliffs, N.J.: Prentice-Hall, 1962, pp. 169-70.

32. *Ibid.*, pp. 173-74.

33. *The Key of Solomon the King*, translated by S.L. MacGregor Mathers. London: G. Redway, 1889.

34. *Ibid.*

35. Israel Regardie, *The Golden Dawn*, vol. 3, pp. 229-38.

36. *Ibid.*

37. 'Invisibility', in *Man, Myth, and Magic*. New York: Marshall Cavendish Corporation, 1975.

38. Theodore Flournoy, *Spiritualism and Psychology*, translated by Hereward Carrington. London: Harper and Bros., 1911, p. 255.

39. Dr J.D. Ward, 'Suspended Animation', *The Rosicrucian Digest*, August 1931, pp. 581-91.

40. Leon H. Zeller, PhD., *Twenty-five Lessons in Hypnotism*. Baltimore: Ottenheimer Publishers, undated, p. 20.

41. *Ibid.*, p. 22.

42. Milton V. Kline and Don Ward, *Favourite Stories of Hypnotism*. Cornwall, N.Y.: Cornwall Press, 1965, p. 213.

43. Harry Arons, *Prize-winning Methods of Hypnosis and Other Simple Induction Techniques*. South Orange, New Jersey: Power Publishers, Inc., 1972, p. 81.

44. Flournoy, p. 255n.

45. Robert W. Marks, *The Story of Hypnotism*. New York: Prentice-Hall, 1947, p. 27.

Chapter 7:

1. William Manchester, *American Caesar.* New York: Dell Publishing Company, 1978, p. 528.

2. Edmund Shaftesbury, *Instantaneous Personal Magnetism.* Meriden, Connecticut: The Ralston Company, 1926, pp. 30-1.

3. Sprenger, *Malleus Maleficarum*, p. 17.

4. *Ibid.*

5. H.P. Blavatsky, *Isis Unveiled*, vol 1, p. xxxii.

6. Plato, *Timaeus*, 45d, translated by Benjamin Jowett, in *Plato: Collected Dialogues.* Princeton University Press, 1973, p. 1173.

7. *Ibid.*

8. Zeller, *A History of Greek Philosophy*, translated by S.F. Alleyne. London: Longmans, Green & Co., 1881, vol 1, p. 166.

9. Aristotle, *Generation of Animals*, translated by A.L. Peck. London: Loeb Classical Library, 1943, p. 495.

10 *Ibid.*, p. 405.

11. Aristotle, *De Sensu*, translated by W.S. Hett, M.A. London: The Loeb Classical Library, 1936, p. 225.

12. Aristotle, *On Dreams*, translated by W.S. Hett, M.A. London: Loeb Classical Library, 1957, p. 356.

13. *Ibid.*, p. 357.

14. Shaftesbury, op. cit., p. 88.

15. *Ibid.*, p. 125.

16. Cornelius Agrippa, quoted by Thomas Vaughan in *Works*, p. 107.

17. Quoted by Israel Regardie, *The Philosopher's Stone.* Saint Paul, Minnesota, 1970, p. 90.

18. Morien of Rome, *A Testament of Alchemy*, p. 27.

19. Hermes, *The Book of the Seven Chapters*, in Atwood's *Suggestive Inquiry.* These texts were first brought together by Titus Burkhardt in his *Alchemy*, translated by William Stoddart. Baltimore: Penguin Books, 1974, p. 24. Burkhardt has a different interpretation, based on a mystical interpretation of alchemy as a whole.

20. Hartmann, *Paracelsus*, p. 296.

21. Dion Fortune, *Psychic Self Defence.* New York: Samuel Weiser, 1979, p. 177.

22. Joseph Weed, *The Wisdom of the Mystic Masters.* West Nyack, New York: Parker Publishing Company, 1968. Weed discusses the *mantra* RA-MA, which is known in Rosicrucian parlance as a 'vowel sound', although he makes no mention of the experiment with the *cloud.*

23. Charles Richet, *Thirty Years of Psychic Research*, p. 491. See also p. 468.

24. Thomas Vaughan, *Works*, p. 193.

25. H.P. Blavatsky, *Isis Unveiled*, vol. 1, pp. 378-79.

Chapter 8:

1. Philostratus, *The Life of Apollonius of Tyana*, translated by F.C. Conybeare. London: The Loeb Classical Library, 1960. Book 3, chapter 13, p. 253.

2. Thomas Vaughan, *Works*, p. 354

3. Philostratus, op. cit., pp. 283 et seq.

4. H.P. Blavatsky, *Isis Unveiled*, vol. 2, p. 597.

5. Dom Pernety, *The Great Art*, p. 76.

6. H.P. Blavatsky, *Isis Unveiled*, vol 1, p. 473.

7. Bonus of Ferrara, *The New Pearl of Great Price*, translated by Arthur Edward Waite. New York: Arno Press, 1974, pp. 187, 225, 231, etc.

8. Op. cit.

9. *Ibid*.

10. Atwood, op. cit.

11. Sir Arthur Conan Doyle, *History of Spiritualism*, p. 114, vol. 2.

12. Jung, *Psychology and Alchemy*, pp. 278-9.

13. John Read, *Through Alchemistry to Chemistry*. London: G. Bell, 1957, p. 25.

14. Franz Hartmann, *Paracelsus*, p. 346.

15. Papus, *La Magie et l'Hypnose*. Paris: Editions Traditionelles, 1975, pp. 232 et seq.

16. H.P. Blavatsky, *Isis Unveiled*, vol. 2, p. 596n.

17. *Ibid*.

18. See the chart on p. 94 of H.P. Blavatsky's *An Abridgement of the Secret Doctrine*, edited by Elizabeth Preston and Christmas Humphreys. London: The Theosophical Publishing House, 1966.

19. Manly Hall, *The Secret Teachings*, pp. cxxvii-cxxviii.

20. *Ibid*., p. cxxvii.

21. Max Müller, *Six Systems of Indian Philosophy*. New York: Longmans, Green & Co., 1899, p. 245

22. *Ibid*., p. 292.

23. *Ibid*., p. 291

24. *Ibid*., p. 283.

25. *Ibid.*, p. 282.

26. *Ibid.*, p. 283.

27. *Ibid.*, p. 291.

28. *Ibid.*, p. 250.

29. *Ibid.*, p. 250.

30. *Ibid.*, pp. 250, 264, 267.

31. *Ibid.*, p. 264.

32. Theos Bernard, *Hindu Philosophy*. New York: The Philosophical Library, 1946, p. 197.

33. *Ibid.*, p. 99.

34. *Ibid.*, p. 197.

35. Maharishi Mahesh Yogi, *On the Bhagavad-Gita*. New York: Penguin Books, 1976, p. 483.

36. Theos Bernard, op. cit., p. 99.

37. Babbitt, *Principles*, p. 341.

38. Müller, op. cit.

39. Bernard, op. cit., p. 101.

40. Rama Prasad, *Nature's Finer Forces*. Adyar, Madras, India: The Theosophical Publishing House, 1933.

41. *Ibid.*

42. Maharishi Mahesh Yogi, p. 483.

43. Rama Prasad, *Patanjali's Yoga Sutras*. Allahabad, 1912.

44. Quoted by Alice Bailey in *The Light of the Soul*. New York: Lucis Publishing Company, 1955, p. 43.

45. Swami Vivekananda, 'Raja Yoga', in *The Complete Works of Swami Vivekananda*. Calcutta: Advaita Ashram, 1971-3, pp. 283-4.

46. *The Siva Samhita*, translated by Srisachandra Vasu. Allahabad, 1914.

47. Patanjali, *Yoga Sutras*, Book 3, Sutra 48. The numbering varies slightly from translation to translation. This numbering is Vivekananda's.

48. Max Müller, p. 285.

49. Theos Bernard, p. 164.

50. Vivekananda, p. 277.

51. W.Y. Evans-Wentz, *The Tibetan Book of the Great Liberation*. London: Oxford University Press, 1972, p. 127.

52. Alice Bailey, p. 281.

53. *Ibid.*, p. 282.

54. Rick Fields, 'Levitation for the Masses', *New Age*, July, 1977, p. 53.

55. David Orme-Johnson, et al., 'Higher States of Consciousness: EEG Coherence, Creativity, and Experience of the Sidhis,' paper 102, *Scientific*

Research on the Transcendental Meditation Program, Collected Papers, Vol. I. MERU Press, p. 708.

56. Karel Werner, *Yoga and Indian Philosophy*. Delhi: Motilal Banarsidass, 1977, p. 81.

57. Vaughan, *Works*, p. 106.

58. *Ibid.*, p. 110.

59. Alexandra David-Neel, *Magic and Mystery in Tibet*. New Hyde Park, New York: University Books, 1965, p. 302.

60. J.H. Brennan, *Experimental Magic*, p. 113.

61. David-Neel, p. 303.

62. Evans-Wentz, *The Tibetan Book*, p. 127.

63. Aleister Crowley, *The Confessions of Aleister Crowley*. New York: Bantam Books, 1971, p. 198.

64. *Ibid.*

65. Eliphas Lévi, *Dogme et Rituel*, pp. 277-8.

66. Aleister Crowley, *Eight Lectures*, p. 68.

67. J.H. Brennan, *Experimental Magic*, p. 114.

Chapter 9:

1. Dion Fortune, *Psychic Self Defence*. New York: Samuel Weiser, 1979, p. 129.

2. H. Spencer Lewis, *Mansions of the Soul*. San Jose, California: The Rosicrucian Press, Ltd., 1930.

3. Israel Regardie, *The Tree of Life*, p. 94.

4. *Ibid.*

5. This view in both Dionysius of Halicarnassus, and in Plutarch: *Isis and Osiris*.

6. *Iamblichus on the Mysteries of the Egyptians, Chaldeans, and Assyrians*, translated by Thomas Taylor. London: Stuart and Watkins, 1968, p. 11.

7. E.A.W. Budge, *The Gods of the Egyptians*. New York: Dover Publications, 1968, vol. 2, p. 469.

8. *Ibid.*, note 6.

9. Eunapius, *Lives of the Sophists*, translated by W.C. Wright. London: The Loeb Classical Library, 1961.

10. *Ibid.*, note 6.

11. *Ibid.*, p. 284.

12. *Ibid.*, p. 285.

13. *Ibid.*, pp. xxiii–xxiv.

14. Dom Pernety, *The Great Art*, pp. 34, 149, 150. The original Latin expression was *nigrum, nigro, nigrius.*

15. Flamel, p. 32.

16. Regardie, p. 244.

17. *Iamblichus*, pp. 286-7.

18. Israel Regardie, *The Golden Dawn*, vol. 3, book 6, pp. 231-2.

19. *Ibid.*, p. 237.

20. *Ibid.*, p. 233.

21. *Ibid.*, p. 237.

22. Crowley, *Confessions*, p. 198.

23. See Chapter Three.

24. Regardie, *The Golden Dawn*, p. 237.

25. *Ibid.*, p. 235.

26. *Ibid.*, p. 236.

27. *Ibid.*, p. 237.

28. *Ibid.*, p. 229.

29. *Ibid.*, p. 146.

30. *The Key of Solomon*, translated by MacGregor Mathers.

31. *Ibid.*

32. *Ibid.*

33. Grillot de Givry, pp. 184-5.

34. Op. cit., p. 200.

35. Israel Regardie, *The Eye in the Triangle*. Saint Paul, Minnesota: Llewellyn Publications, 1970, p. 241.

36. Regardie, *The Golden Dawn*, p. 236.

37. *Ibid.*, pp. 233, 234, 236.

38. *Ibid.*, vol. 1, p. 194.

39. Eliphas Lévi, *Philosophe Occulte*, quoted by Mathers in *The Key of Solomon*, which see.

40. Mathers, *The Book of the Sacred Magic*, p. 200.

41. Regardie, *The Golden Dawn*, vol. 1, p. 194.

42. *Ibid.*, vol. 3, p. 230.

43. *Ibid.*, pp. 174-5.

44. *Ibid.*, pp. 237-8.

45. Op. cit., p. 245.

46. Op. cit., p. 124.

47. Op. cit., p. 135.

48. *Ibid.*, p. 141n.

49. *Ibid.*, p. 142n.

59. *Ibid.*

51. *Ibid.*, pp. 134-5n.

52. *The Mahatma Letters to A.P. Sinnet*, transcribed and compiled by A.T. Barker, Adyar, Madras, India: The Theosophical Publishing House, 1962, p. 106; also Hartmann's *Paracelsus*, p. 128n.

53. W.Y. Evans-Wentz, *The Tibetan Book of the Dead*. Oxford University Press, 1960.

54. *Ibid.*

Index